They Call Me Little Willie
The Life Story of William L. Adams

Mark R. Cheshire

ISBN: 0615707165
ISBN-13: 978-0615707167

DEDICATION

To the woman who cultivated my love of books
— my grandmother, Louise.

CONTENTS

001 THE RECKONING

With Sunday night about to turn into Monday morning, William Lloyd Adams finally pulled his new Ford to the curb in Sugar Hill, the nicest of Baltimore City's all-black neighborhoods, and switched off the motor. The drive had been long — nearly 400 miles round-trip — but well worth it. Along with his wife Victorine, he had gone to Pompton Lakes, New Jersey, a usually sleepy, all-white town roughly 30 miles outside of New York City, to watch his good friend train for the most highly anticipated sporting event in history.

In less than two weeks, Joe Louis, the former heavyweight champion, would get the opportunity to avenge his only loss against the current champion, Max Schmeling. Interest in their June 1938 rematch ran deep. In addition to being the biggest stars in one of the world's most popular sports, Louis and Schmeling also were widely perceived as proxies for two countries, America and Germany, hurtling toward a second calamitous war. People on both sides of the Atlantic Ocean followed the fighters' every move — every skip of the jump rope and every jumping jack — with a patriotic fervor. And the fight had yet another layer of meaning and significance for many black Americans. Only in the boxing ring, Malcolm X later observed, could a black man kick the ass of white man without being arrested or worse.

Seeing the Brown Bomber defeat white opponents exhilarated many who were beaten down daily, figuratively and literally. Conversely, the sight terrified countless whites. They worried that the image of a black hitting a white would foment an uprising. As a result, some white movie theater operators refused to show the immensely popular newsreel footage of Louis bouts. They broke with policy, however, when Schmeling defeated Louis.

For these reasons, Louis's training session on Sunday, June 12, 1938, drew some 9,000 people. This despite the fact that tickets sold for $1.10 at a time when the average weekly salary stood at roughly $20. Even teachers, who were among the better-paid professionals, earned just $26.42 a week on average in 1938. Those who couldn't afford tickets sneaked in or scaled nearby buildings and sat on the rooftops to catch a glimpse of the action. Fearful of injuries or even a roof collapse, organizers installed barbed wire in time for the Louis's final public preparations the following weekend. On the wooden benches surrounding the outdoor ring, whites and blacks wedged themselves tightly together, shoulder to shoulder, the regular rules of segregated seating clearly relaxed for the special occasion.

The crowd watched ravenously as Louis performed calisthenics and sparred for six uneventful rounds.

Although he enjoyed the spectacle, Adams preferred a different type of round with Louis.

Separated in age by just four months, Adams and Louis got together the previous year at Carroll Park, Baltimore's only colored golf course. In addition to a mutual love of the game, they shared a great deal in common. Both grew up fatherless and desperately poor in the Jim Crow South. Both joined the Great Migration, during which roughly seven million blacks abandoned the dead-end and deadly South and relocated to northern cities, hoping to secure better jobs and lives. Both possessed what writer Richard Wright would soon describe in his classic novel "Native Son" as a "gnawing hunger and restless aspiration." And both men, defying monumentally long odds rigged by racism, harnessed that drive to produce fairytale success stories and prodigious earnings. But on this Sunday, the two 24-year-old men shared something more profound than cash and cachet. They both were in real jeopardy of losing it all, although Adams didn't yet know it. He would soon.

As William and Victorine got out of the car and headed to the front door of their building, William quickly surveyed the activity around the building's side door, the entrance to his first-floor nightclub, Little Willie's Inn. Although he preferred for strategic reasons to keep a low profile in most aspects of his life and work, Adams used his own nickname for the establishment. It would have made little sense to do otherwise. By this time, the name "Little Willie" represented more than the man. It also encapsulated his reputation for incomparable reliability and absolute devotion to the improvement of the black race. Those who knew Adams, those who sought and received his generous support, revered him. Not surprisingly, Little Willie's Inn immediately emerged as one of the most popular black nightspots in the city. But on this night, business lagged. Sundays typically proved to be among the busiest days of the week. Most people fortunate enough to have jobs during the second wave of the Great Depression put in five-and-a-half-day work weeks, with payday falling on the half day of Saturday. Sundays, therefore, served as their only full day of respite. Responding to demand, Little Willie's frequently hosted two musical performances on Sundays rather than the usual one. A few blocks away, a competing nightclub presented three performances on Sundays, the first starting at 6 a.m., the last blowing all the way until closing time at 2 a.m. But for whatever reason, Little Willie's Inn drew so sparse a crowd on this Sunday that the club's manager, Joseph Quille, William's father-in-law, sent his final waitress home earlier than usual and turned his attention to closing the club. As he did so, his daughter and son-in-law prepared for bed upstairs in their third-floor apartment.

Victorine turned in first. A teacher at School No. 103, the all-black school down the street, she had a busy day ahead of her, as always. William expected to be similarly busy but in a conspicuously different line of work. In terms of education and profession, the couple served as a study in contrasts. Victorine had earned a college degree, a rare attainment at a time when only five percent of the total population held a bachelor's degree. Despite the accomplishment, the color of her skin rendered her ineligible for all but three professions: education, law, and medicine. For William, armed only with a seventh graduation, and an inferior one at that, the options were few and unappealing.

Not satisfied with the prospects of a life of physical labor, he forged his own path, a path that made him a man of great interest to politicians, police, prosecutors, and the criminal underground. Adams headed a growing illegal gambling ring, and he, too, needed to hit the streets early. Despite his success, he refused to relax. Few journeys, he knew, are easier to complete than the one from riches to rags. Stop working, start indulging, and the money will disappear, quickly. After climbing a few rungs up the financial ladder, too many people abandoned the effort that propelled their ascent and adopted lavish lifestyles adorned with elegant clothes and exquisite cars. Not Adams. He had worked too hard and come too far. He was less than 10 years removed from picking cotton for a penny a pound. If poverty ever reclaimed him, it would not be the result of indolence. Nor would it come as a consequence of hubris. He knew that his primary business was precarious. Arrest always loomed as an imminent threat to his life and livelihood, as did competition from violent gangsters who were looking for new ways to generate revenue now that the repeal of Prohibition had dried up their illegal alcohol enterprises. What's more, he didn't want to be a criminal. He longed to be a legitimate businessman. Crime was a means to an end, one of the only means that a minority could tap to generate enough capital to launch a business career.

For his first foray into legal business, Adams selected real estate. At a time when just 17 percent of Baltimore's black families owned their home, Adams owned several. The remaining 83 percent rented, usually from white landlords, paying a median monthly price of $25.25, a sum so great that a third of them were forced to take on lodgers to make ends meet. Indeed, the devastating combination of racism and economic depression proved inordinately deleterious to the black community. While the federal government did not yet measure poverty, historians later determined that 90 percent of the black community lived below the poverty line by the close of the 1930s. By contrast, when Adams bought the building that hosted his home and business in 1936, the first thing he did was secure city approval and knock down the two-story structure. On the site, he paid for the construction of one of the largest and most well-appointed buildings in the area. Instead of two stories, he built three. He also extended the building's footprint, and developed four apartments on the second and third floors featuring high-end amenities that even many whites couldn't afford, such as showers. By contrast, less than a third of houses in his Sugar Hill neighborhood even had bathtubs.

He also invested great sums of cash and care to prepare Little Willie's Inn for business. Of course he wanted to make money, but that wasn't his only objective with the nightclub. He was disgusted by the dismal quality of entertainment venues that admitted blacks, almost all of them owned by whites. Because of segregation, blacks out for a night on the town had no choice but to accept the inferior conditions. Adams spent generously to create an exception. The black community reciprocated Adams's care with their patronage, as well as with their devotion and admiration.

Just after 3 a.m., Joseph Quille locked the door to Little Willie's Inn as his daughter and son-in-law were dozing off to sleep upstairs. But within a matter of minutes, an explosion shattered the early morning quiet. The sound and force of the eruption were heard and felt throughout the city, prompting a deluge of frightened telephone calls to the police department. They called from the neighborhood surrounding Johns Hopkins Hospital three miles to the east and from Key Highway, a ship repair district five miles to the south, among other places. What's happening, they pleaded? Some of the dramatic answers to their questions would become public within a matter of hours. Others took longer to uncover. But the most important question of all would go unanswered.

Until now.

002 THE KID FROM KINGS MOUNTAIN

The improbable story of William Adams began in a place with a name that is at once perfectly fitting and cruelly ironic. Seven months before the start of World War I, Adams was born on January 5, 1914, in Kings Mountain, North Carolina. While he would come to be widely regarded as near-royalty in the black community years later, his birth and childhood were anything but regal. Adams never knew his father. Later in life, he claimed the man died when he was just a boy. His mother, Claudia, who was 22 at the time of his birth, all but abandoned him at the age of four. She paid an occasional Christmas day visit to her son and daughter, but nothing more. Not until adulthood did he learn the surprising truth about his absent parents, a truth he shared with few others.

Even his closest friends and associates never knew that Adams's father was white. Claudia served as his maid. A search of local records and newspapers produced nothing to supplement the scant account delivered to Adams by his mother's brother, Reather. Adams's father was a prominent businessman who died in the mid-1940s, Reather said.

Considering the time and place of his birth, it is not unreasonable to wonder whether Adams was the product of a consensual relationship or barbarism. During slavery, it was legal and tragically common for white men to ravage their black servants. The Thirteenth Amendment to the Constitution may have officially ended slavery 48 years before Adams was conceived, but many of slavery's deplorable customs lived on.

However, the only available account suggests a different explanation. On at least one occasion, Adams's father held his newborn son in his hands with pride, according to Adams's uncle. Circumstances surrounding his mother's relocation lend some support to the theory that his father was, at the very least, a benign figure, and perhaps, hopefully, something more, something better. Claudia stayed in Kings Mountain for four years following the birth of her son. The father easily could have made such a stay untenable. He could have blocked her every opportunity at making even a modest living. Even if he was a good man with genuine feelings for Adams's mother, he would have had a compelling reason to force her and their son out of town. Interracial relationships were illegal in 1914, and remained so in North Carolina until the Supreme Court's landmark *Loving v. Virginia* miscegenation ruling in 1967. What's more, the risk of prosecution and imprisonment was relatively insignificant compared to the punishment that some in the racist white community could — and did — administer. In what was a relatively slow year for such atrocities, 51 blacks were lynched in 1914. The number surged to 76 four years later.

But not until 1918 did Claudia leave Kings Mountain, moving across the state to Winston-Salem to take a job in the burgeoning cigarette industry. In that same year, she also left four-year-old William, turning him and his seven-year-old sister, Luvenia, over to her parents to raise in a town called Zebulon. William's biological father provided Claudia and her parents with cash and a cow, either as a gesture of support for his son or as means to persuade Claudia to leave. Either way, William's grandparents, whom Adams would come to regard as his parents, desperately needed whatever support they could get.

The couple lived in a home with no electricity or plumbing, relying on a woodstove to keep warm and prepare what food there was to eat. The cow, Dolly, which William cared for, provided the family's milk. William's grandfather, Ernest, labored as an illiterate sharecropper. His grandmother, who went by the name Willie, tended to the home and children. While uneducated, Willie could read, a relatively rare skill at the time. She shared her ability with others by teaching Sunday school at nearby Wakefield Baptist Church. The family's dire and unrelieved poverty didn't register with William. It was all he knew. He'd never seen or heard of anything else. And it was absolutely everywhere. Poverty didn't discriminate in Zebulon, claiming the hope and vitality of whites just as mercilessly as it did that of blacks. Penury pre-empted any questions that might have otherwise arisen about how best to rear a young boy. As a male, he went to work in the fields with his grandfather. Just like the grown men, young William worked long, grueling days picking cotton and tobacco to help his family fulfill its obligation to the white man who owned not only the fields, but also their house and the general store where they bought supplies that they couldn't grow or produce themselves.

After the fall picking season, tenant farmers and the owner met for the so-called "settle." In concept, the settle was simple. In practice, it was anything but. The owner weighed and declared the price he would pay for the sharecropper's harvest. From that sum, he withheld what the sharecropper owed him for the use of the land and home. He also required payment at this time for the merchandise the sharecropper purchased at the store on credit throughout the year. The objective for sharecroppers, of course, was to walk away from the settle with cash. If a tenant farmer strung together a number of successful years and saved his profits, then he could buy a home and field of his own and thereby escape sharecropping, which was a direct and not-so-distant descendant of slavery and forced servitude. With four mouths to feed, Ernest absolutely needed William's labor to stand any chance of liberating his family from the arrangement. Schooling had to be secondary, if it was to be pursued at all. But even with his grandson's dogged contribution, Ernest failed year after year to produce the profit necessary to slip the bonds of sharecropping. He walked away from the settle with too little or, worse, with a bill for an outstanding balance, which bound him and his family to the owner for another season. This annual failure cultivated a fervid bitterness in the heart of William's grandmother, a bitterness that she couldn't help but pass on to her grandchildren. Willie didn't blame the owner or the system of sharecropping. She blamed her husband, Adams recalled decades later.

It wasn't that Ernest was lazy. In fact, he toiled like an animal and produced enough crops to get them out of sharecropping, she felt. The problem was his ignorance. His illiteracy and inability to calculate numbers made him easy prey for the unscrupulous. Cotton buyers could and did lie to him about how much cotton he delivered for sale. Unable to read the weight registered on the scale, he was at their mercy. In truth, Willie's harsh criticism was at least somewhat unfair. The sharecropping system was all but designed to keep tenant farmers from earning their way out. Owners typically charged too much for supplies and paid too little for their crops. And if a sharecropper mustered the courage to protest, then the white owner could easily employ physical means to enforce compliance, and do so with impunity. Making matters worse, the so-called roaring 1920s, marked by exponential economic gains for some, left the agricultural industry in the dust. Following the completion of World War I, farmers resumed their work in the fields, producing surpluses that sent prices plunging. Cotton, for example, tumbled by more than half from 35 cents per pound during the war to 16 cents in 1920. The crisis persisted throughout the 1920s, growing so dire that President Herbert Hoover, a free-market conservative, called a special legislative session that resulted in the passage of the Agricultural Marketing Act of 1929. Under the bill, government-sponsored "stabilization corporations" bought surplus products to prop up prices.

Nevertheless, Willie seethed, convinced that her husband was responsible for their privations. She passed her unrelieved frustration on to her grandson, along with one very urgent plea: Above all else, she implored her grandson, learn how to count. If you know how to handle the math that underlies all financial transactions, you'll always be in a position of power, she said. Nobody will ever be able to take advantage of you. The woman's words made an impression on William that lasted a lifetime.

When he became eligible at the age of six to attend the local colored school, William set about mastering mathematics with a monomaniacal focus. When the teacher presented English or history lessons, Adams would restlessly bide his time, waiting for the subject of his deliverance. Adams particularly liked to engage in chalkboard math competitions against classmates. The teacher would give them problems and the race was on to determine who was the fastest and most accurate. More than 70 years later, Adams could still recall with ease the names of the students who challenged him for math supremacy: Andrew Hall and Wydell Barnes. Barnes was the fastest, Adams conceded. But Adams claimed the distinction of most accurate. He was proud of his development, but he would ultimately grow frustrated by the disparity in the way blacks and whites were educated. The colored school was open only six months per year, the white school nine months.

It was also around this time that Adams developed a very favorable taste for the buying power of money. He wanted candy, which was well beyond his grandparents' means. So after working with his grandfather and attending school, he started to pick up odd jobs. Still less than 10 years old, Adams demonstrated a precocious ability to identify money-making opportunities. For example, after the fall harvest, cotton plants retained small pieces of hard-to-get cotton. Even the poorest sharecroppers dismissed it as too little and too difficult to collect. Not Adams. He picked the remnants from every field where he could gain admission, traveling as far as three miles from his home on foot to do so. He then identified a cotton gin operator in Zebulon willing to buy the scraps and delivered to him regularly. For his efforts throughout the region, Adams earned the nickname Cotton Field Willie. He also earned enough money to enter a new line of business — bicycle repair.

A broken bike was a big deal for those struggling to make ends meet. Few could afford to pay the bicycle shop owner to handle the repair or knew how to make the fix themselves. So Adams learned how to order replacement parts through the mail from Montgomery Ward and return the bikes to operability. This enabled him to make money in two ways. He could lure customers by making repairs for less than the bike shop charged, or he could buy the broken bikes outright, rehab them, and then resell them to those able to meet his price. His success in this led to yet another business. Grocery stores relied heavily on bike deliveries. By being able to repair his own means of transportation, Adams quickly emerged as the most reliable delivery boy in the area and consequently secured a steady stream of work. All of these endeavors financed more than his candy habit. Although just a boy, Adams was almost entirely self-sufficient, paying for his own clothes and shoes and helping with his family's bills.

Adams saw that other kids his age spent more of their free time playing baseball and hunting. He found time for this, too. But he devoted most of his energy to work. Having to forgo childhood recreation for adulthood responsibility didn't make Adams sullen or resentful, as it easily could have. In fact, he was enlivened by it. He saw first-hand that hard work and determination could produce a better life. The truth is, he loved his life in Zebulon. He loved to work and learn. And above all else, he loved his grandmother. But that life came to a devastating end when his grandmother died in 1929. Adams was free to stay in Zebulon with his grandfather, but that was unacceptable to him. He shared his grandmother's profound frustration with the man. Without her, there was no hope that the family would ever make any progress, he felt. They would just remain forever trapped by the man's ignorance. Adams's biological mother encouraged the children to rejoin her. But William rejected the offer. The woman whom he recognized as his true mother was dead. Instead, he and his sister elected to accept their uncle's invitation to move to Baltimore City and live with his family. After helping his grandfather complete the fall harvest and the settle, Adams, uncertain and elegiac, boarded a segregated train car bound for the north. For the second time in his 15-year-old life, William Adams had to start all over again.

003 BALTIMORE BEGINNINGS

Shortly after the stock market's vertiginous plunge in 1929, Adams stepped off the train in Baltimore. The teen-ager had never seen a city before, and now, suddenly, he lived in one. The frenetic swirl of activity reminded him of a beehive. Everything and everyone seemed to be moving with great speed and purpose. This, he thought, is a place of possibility. His first impression, so full of romance and optimism, wouldn't last long.

Just 15 years old and unemployed, William had no choice but to move into his Uncle Reather's tiny East Baltimore apartment. Home to Reather's growing brood of children, the place was already overcrowded, but they made the best of it, cramming several kids into bedrooms suitable for only one or two. School was out of the question. Adams had to pay his way, just as Reather's children did, so, within one week of arriving in town, William sought and secured a job where his cousins worked: a company that prepared old rags for shipment to foreign buyers who converted the material into paper in most cases. William spent five and half days every week stomping on rags with his feet to squeeze as many as possible into shipping crates, a process that filled the waterfront warehouse with fumes and dust. Not only did the acrid air make it hard for workers to breathe. It also gave them reason to fear for their lives. Tuberculosis, a deadly bacterial infection that spreads through the air, was rampant in the 1930s, claiming more lives than any other contagious disease. So lethal and widespread was the disease that it earned an ominous moniker: "the great white plague." At the time, skinny people were considered particularly vulnerable, and Adams was definitely skinny, weighing just 104 pounds. The prospect of infection and death was more than an abstraction for Adams. His younger cousin had already died of the disease.

Adams seriously considered moving back to North Carolina. His new situation was awful. His uncle's house was cramped. The workplace was potentially lethal, and for his dangerous labor he earned just $6 a week, less than he made in the South. Making matters even worse, Baltimore was rife with a sort of racism Adams had never experienced before. Back home in Zebulon, he had played with and worked for whites. In Baltimore, whites rarely deigned to consort with or hire blacks. And when they did, they openly expressed their disregard and even hatred. For Adams, the bigotry was more than painful and demeaning. It was also profoundly discouraging. He had come to believe that life in a northern city would be better, more equitable, for Negroes like himself. That great promise appeared to be a lie. It was just as the poet Langston Hughes had written in

"Po' Boy Blues." "When I was home de/sunshine seemed like gold./Since I come up North de/whole damn world's turned cold." But there was nowhere else for Adams to go. There was no home to which he could return. He had to figure out how to forge a better future for himself right where he was. Others struggled similarly. For example, despite having graduated from college, Thurgood Marshall, a future Supreme Court justice, could not find a job to support himself in his hometown of Baltimore, either. As a result, he decided to go back to what he was doing before college: waiting tables at an all-white country club. Adams quickly regained his resolve and turned to what he already did best. He looked for a better opportunity to seize.

With workers plentiful and jobs increasingly scarce as the nation plunged inexorably into a depression, white business owners had even less incentive to hire black individuals for anything but the most menial jobs, such as those at the rag warehouse. Baltimore was then home to more blacks than any other northern city, and few of them had been able to cobble together the money to open a business of their own and create jobs for others. Adams, however, found one. It was bicycle shop run by a man from North Carolina whose name Adams would never forget, and for good reason. Johnny Wiggins shrewdly set up his operation in Fells Point, a popular destination for newly arrived immigrants from countries where bicycles played a central role in daily life. By 1930, 30 percent of the U.S. population was made up of individuals either born in a foreign country or having at least one foreign-born parent. Impressed with Adams's ability to assemble bikes and spoke tires, Wiggins hired him, despite his surprising youth. For a time, the two flourished together. Wiggins went out into the streets and drummed up business while Adams did the work back at the shop. They sold refurbished bikes for $8 to $10, depending on the make and model. While working for Wiggins, Adams built a bike for himself, which he routinely pedaled more than seven miles each way to Dr. Thomas's Beach at Turner Station, the only public beach that permitted black visitors.

But within a matter of months, unemployment surged to a staggering 20 percent. Without the financial safety net of unemployment insurance, people were forced to slash expenditures. In no time, bicycles turned from a necessary mode of transportation to an inaccessible luxury. With great despair, Wiggins had no choice but to lay off Adams and try to make a go of it on his own. But having established a close relationship with his young charge, Wiggins was determined to do whatever he could to help Adams find a replacement job, and Adams, once again, had an idea.

His uncle's landlord lived directly below Adams and Reather's family. Unable to read, she routinely asked Adams to help her with the morning newspaper. Adams had mastered reading back in North Carolina by perusing the newspaper his grandmother received, the *Gastonia Gazette*. The landlady wasn't interested in the day's headlines about the economy or President Hoover. Instead, she wanted him to decipher an obscure set of numbers buried in the agate type. She wanted to know if she was a winner. She explained, to Adams's astonishment, that there was money to be won or lost on the numbers published in the paper. A man would soon come by to take her one-penny bet. If she accurately predicted tomorrow's three-digit number, then he would return the following day with her winnings: $6. Adams's mind teemed with questions, not unlike the math problems he had solved on the chalkboard back in Zebulon. How could someone wager just one penny on three numbers and collect $6? Who could afford that proposition? Better yet, what was in it for the man who paid off the bet? He eventually solved the problem, reasoning that the odds of selecting the winning number weren't very good. If a person collected enough losing bets, he could afford to pay off the occasional winner and still have cash left over for himself.

When Wiggins offered to help him find a new job, Adams didn't hesitate. I want to run numbers, he declared. Wiggins expressed deep skepticism. The numbers racket was illegal and best left to adults. Players and runners often found themselves in trouble with the law and in violent disputes. That's too much for a 16-year-old to handle. But Adams made a strong case, arguing that his mastery of math would make him less susceptible to fraud and other schemes that bedeviled less knowledgeable runners. He also asked Wiggins to consider the reliability and honesty that he had demonstrated during his time working at the bike shop. Wiggins relented, but he knew that big-time numbers operators wouldn't take a flyer on Adams without his personal backing. Wiggins dutifully ushered Adams to the biggest numbers operation in East Baltimore, the Six and Eight Company.

Although the numbers were against the law, Six and Eight operated overtly, a bold sign hanging over the front door, the owners seemingly unconcerned about a police raid. Like almost all of the other numbers businesses, Six and Eight was owned and operated by whites. As Wiggins predicted, a boss at the enterprise quickly rejected Adams. Too young. Can't be trusted to do the necessary math and handle the cash reliably for all involved. If a runner stole or mishandled money, then Six and Eight would pay twice. It would lose the revenue and yet be forced to pay off winners or risk having those players find someone else with whom to do business. Despite his own mounting financial difficulties, Wiggins made Six and Eight a promise: If Adams fails and loses money for you, I'll pay you back in full. I guarantee this young man, he said. And so, Adams became a numbers runner.

004 ENTRY-LEVEL RACKETEER

Adams may have had a backer in Johnny Wiggins and an employer in Six & Eight, but he didn't have customers. This was no small matter. While players in Baltimore were plentiful, a new runner couldn't poach a competitor's regulars without consequences. There were boundaries to observe and respect. The city's west side, for instance, appeared to be completely off limits. Thomas R. Smith, Baltimore's only Negro political machine boss and therefore the most powerful black man in town, dominated that section of town. Known as "The Chief," Smith controlled jobs, housing, churches, police, politicians, and everything else, all of which he could bring to bear on someone who encroached on any of his business enterprises, such as his numbers operation, Lucky Numbers.

The east side of the city where Adams lived was not under the control of a single boss. It was fragmented, with several powerful figures and several significant numbers operations, including Six & Eight. To keep the peace and prevent costly price wars, leaders of the established numbers rackets colluded. They fixed the prices to be paid to winners and workers, and they divided the market, block by city block, agreeing not to pursue customers outside of their designated territories. Consequently, all of the established east side rackets offered bettors the same payout ratio, usually 600 to one, and they all paid their runners the same rate of commission. Runners typically received 20 percent of their gross collections. Not surprisingly, considering the millions to be made pedaling numbers, outsiders and upstarts inevitably tried to move in on the established rackets. But, just as inevitably, such attempts were quickly thwarted, and almost always without violence, the reason being that the illegal operators bribed the police to protect themselves not only from arrest but also from unacknowledged competitors. In no time, intruders would find themselves under police surveillance or arrest, with information provided by the established criminals. Corrupt cops and officials were highly motivated. If they failed to deliver both types of protection, they would lose their lucrative side business. What's more, if violence flared, citizens would surely open the blind eye they turned on numbers as long as the illegal gambling didn't put their lives in any danger. The numbers were no secret. Everyone knew that such gambling was flourishing in Baltimore. If the public was provoked to pay attention, it wouldn't take long for someone to wonder: Why aren't the police making more arrests? This would lead to more uncomfortable questions and possibly an investigation. Keeping things peaceful and quiet was critical to all involved, and they were able to pull it off — at least for a time.

In the meantime, the most ambitious numbers runners faced the challenge of distinguishing themselves and securing more business in a rigged market, where everybody sold the same exact product for the same exact price. Also known as writers, runners served as the conduits between customers and what were called the banks — operations such as Six & Eight that took bets, paid winners, and managed the money, employees, police, and other useful public officials. A runner might strike a quiet side deal with customers: place all of your wagers with me and I'll personally supplement your winnings when the time comes. But not many runners were willing and able to part with their own money. And by doing so, they would risk drawing the attention of the bank bosses.

The challenge for Adams was exacerbated by his youth. Players were wary of dealing with a young kid. After all, the numbers weren't just an idle, inconsequential entertainment. The pennies people wagered didn't come easily, and collecting $6 on a winning ticket represented a major windfall, one that enabled players to make ends meet. There weren't many ways for people mired in the Depression to generate $6 without devoting hard labor to earn it, and there weren't many opportunities to do even that. The numbers, then, were serious business for players. Some went so far as to invest in dream books, which were instruction manuals to help people to identify winning numbers embedded in the imagery of their dreams. If someone dreamed a winner and the runner failed to show that day, the dream was squandered. Likewise if a player hit and the runner skipped on the payout. As a result, players wanted to deal with runners who were as reliable as preachers, if not more so. Could they really trust a young man with this responsibility? Adams not only recognized and understood the hurdles he faced. He also devised a strategy to overcome them.

Having been in Baltimore for less than one year, he still didn't know many people. But those he did know had developed a favorable impression of him. A group of men gathered every day outside of Johnny Wiggins's bike shop when Adams worked there. Unemployed, they had nothing else to do but stand around, talk, place the occasional bet when they had a penny to spare, and watch the world around them. Adams was one of the people they watched. He was never late. He never missed a day. And he never made excuses for why something couldn't be done. He produced reliable results, day after day. So when Adams entered the numbers, they didn't need to be convinced to place their wagers with him. They knew that he was responsible and that their bets with him were effectively insured by Wiggins.

Adams did not disappoint. He collected and delivered with greater punctuality than other runners with whom they had dealt in the past. Word of Adams's reliability spread, and so did Adams, having already laid the groundwork for expansion. During his time at the Wiggins's shop, Adams built himself a bicycle for just such an opportunity. As he had back in North Carolina, Adams put the bike to work. While most runners couldn't afford vehicles and therefore conducted business on foot, Adams did so on wheels, which enabled him to cover more territory in less time.

Adams had already come to understand that greater

volume was the key to his success. Like other runners, Adams earned 20 percent of the bets he collected. The bank retained 40 percent, and the balance went to winners. However, he soon discovered, while turning in his numbers at the Six & Eight office, that some runners were paid 25 cents on the dollar. He learned that those writers had sub-writers; that is, they managed other people and therefore got paid a larger percentage because they were bringing in more business. While pedaling his bike one day, Adams decided he had the skills and drive to expand.

Still just 16 years old, Adams went in search of people to hire, a process he undertook with a precocious amount of managerial insight and care for someone so young and inexperienced. While there was an unprecedented surplus of men seeking work, Adams was highly selective. To qualify, a person needed three attributes: an established reputation for honesty and reliability, a strong command of mathematics, and a genuine hunger to do more than earn a mere salary. He would not compromise on any one of these principles. He understood that a dishonest or unreliable employee could, and probably would, demolish the good reputation he was working so hard to build, and that without that sterling reputation his future would be limited at best. He also knew from first-hand experience that even an honest, hard-working man was no good to him unless he could handle the math. His grandfather could never work hard enough to overcome his inability to accurately compute numbers. And finally, Adams was developing a higher-order understanding of human motivation and the business world. He wasn't interested in people who just wanted to earn a few dollars. He wanted people who shared his insatiable appetite for building successful business ventures, and not just for getting rich, although that was one of his many objectives.

Adams was growing increasingly frustrated by the economic system that prevailed in the colored community. Whites owned most of the homes and all of the businesses. Negroes had little choice but to spend their money with white business owners, who in turn invested the proceeds in their white communities. Black money went down a white drain that perpetuated black poverty. If blacks could start building successful businesses, Adams reasoned, then black money would stay in black communities and start to lift everyone out of poverty. What's more, successful business ownership offered a type of freedom. No longer would a proprietor be subject to the whims or even malevolence of white employers. The black business owner would rise or fall on his own merits. And if these were the terms of the game, Adams was very confident about his prospects. Even better, a Negro business owner could hire others, circumventing the system of segregation and provide relative security. And that's exactly what Adams did, making the first hires of his life.

"I decided early that I would do whatever I had to to make money, as long as no one got hurt and I could treat people the way I liked to be treated myself," he told a *Washington Post* reporter more than three decades later. And make money he did. At just 18 years of age, he had earned and saved enough to buy a candy store a few blocks north of Johns Hopkins Hospital in the 1800 block of East Eager Street. In addition to candy, the store sold two-cent shaved ices and offered shoe shine services. While making money was an integral part of the formula for success, so was saving. Between the ages of 16 and 18, he limited his personal spending to just $1.40 per week. At age 19, he acquired another business, a three-chair barbershop. Adams's friends joked about his unwillingness to spend more freely, calling him stingy. As many of them would soon discover, a yawning chasm existed between stingy and frugality, at least for Adams.

005 WHAT'S IN A NICKNAME?

Adams's name and operation spread quickly. Around the time he marked his one-year anniversary in Baltimore, he prepared to buy something inaccessible to almost everyone, white or black: a car. He initially wanted to purchase a motorcycle, having grown accustomed to working on a bicycle, but his uncle convinced him that it was too dangerous. So he settled on a used 1928 Ford featuring one of the latest innovations: an internal starter rather than an external crank. His uncle advised Adams on the purchase even though he couldn't afford a car himself. The automobile immediately set Adams apart. The man who went on to become Baltimore's first black mayor in the 1980s, Clarence "Du" Burns, recalled years later what a thrill it was as a poor black kid seeing another black kid driving an automobile and running a successful enterprise. Adams's peers idolized him, viewing him as a role model despite the fact that he was actually their age or even younger, Burns said.

Like so many other blacks, Adams moved north in pursuit of the American dream. Like them, he had been dirt poor and poorly educated. Like them, he had struggled, tenuously holding a futureless job and facing racial discrimination day after day. But unlike them, he was figuring out how to greatly improve his station in life. Even better, he was beginning to demonstrate an interest in helping other blacks do the same.

However, the more Adams analyzed the world and people around him, the more concerned he became about the professional prospects for his fellow Negroes. It didn't take him long to discover that blacks were involved in scores of business initiatives, legal and otherwise. But he also perceived a disturbing trend. Too many black entrepreneurs flamed out like meteors. Promising starts were too frequently followed by swift, precipitous failures. To be sure, some simply squandered their opportunities by concentrating on spending, rather than earning, money.

Others stalled due to a lack of capital. Financial institutions wouldn't lend to Negroes, and there was only one black man in town with sufficient resources to make meaningful loans: the political boss Tom Smith. If Smith rejected the request, black business people were left to bet on numbers and hope for the best. But in most cases, neglect and liquidity were secondary matters. Adams was coming to understand that Negroes were coming up short for more complicated reasons — and he considered himself similarly vulnerable. The problem was a lack of skill, expertise, and the experience needed to get beyond the start-up phase. A person could get something up and running by relying almost exclusively on hustle and determination. But as the operation matured, more sophisticated quantitative and managerial skills were required, and few Negroes had either. It wasn't just a lack of higher education. In fact, relatively few people attended colleges and universities during the first third of the 20th century. Although enrollment doubled between 1920 and 1930, from 600,000 to 1.2 million, still just 12 percent of 18- to 21-year-olds were attending a higher institution of learning in 1928. The more common way of learning these skills was through formal and informal apprenticeships, a practice that effectively perpetuated the business dominance of whites. If whites trained only whites, then blacks had few places to turn because there were so few established black business leaders. To break the vicious cycle, the colored community needed black business pioneers, Adams concluded.

Less apparent was the question of entrepreneurial drive. Adams struggled to understand the deficiency in others because for him it was innate. It was as much a part of him as the hair on his head. It is what drove him to pick the cotton fields after all the others quit. It's what prompted him to refurbish and resell bicycles, and to use one of them to become a trusted delivery boy in North Carolina. And it is what fueled him to enter the numbers and then expand. Regardless, the younger Adams was convinced that others could match and even surpass him, provided they identified an opportunity, pursued it with zeal, vanquished any uncertainty, and, most importantly, devoted themselves to a life of learning so they would be prepared to take on ever-more sophisticated endeavors.

While Adams devoted most his time to work, he also

made time for play. He was, after all, just a teen-ager with a burgeoning interest in girls. Along with a friend, Charles Tilghman, who would go on to be one of leading nightclub impresarios in Baltimore, Adams attended house parties. The entertainment consisted of a wind-up record player and an improvised dance floor. For the most part, Adams chose to stand on the sidelines, listening to music rather than dancing. He said he wasn't a good enough dancer to keep up with the up-tempo songs. But when the music turned slow, he somehow found the skill — and a partner. It wasn't difficult. He was handsome, built like a long-distance runner, roughly 5 feet 7 inches tall and lean. His eyes, always full of purpose, peered out from a handsome face with a complexion as light as balsa. Light skin was widely coveted, so much so that black newspapers at the time were filled with advertisements hawking skin-bleaching formulas. For instance, an ad for Dr. Fred palmer's Skin Whitener, published in the *Baltimore Afro-American*, asked readers: "Have you been missing out on the fun and pleasures of life unnecessarily because of a too-dark toned surface skin?" For just 25 cents, the company offered to deliver a product that acts fasts "to help nature replace darker, outer skin with brighter under skin." But appearance wasn't all that Adams had going for himself. Smart, driven, and already going places, Adams was a catch, but not one of his dancing partners was able to lure him into anything lasting. That wouldn't come for five more years.

Adams and his friends also liked to go to the movies, although they had to sit in the colored-only section. It was during one of these outings that Adams picked up his nickname. Widely credited with launching the gangster film genre, the 1931 production "Little Caesar," starring Edward G. Robinson, tells the story of a hustler who through hard work and determination climbs to the top of a criminal organization. The similarity between the fictional character Rico and the real-life William Adams wasn't lost on Adams's friends. Shortly after leaving the movie theater, they proposed the moniker "Little Willie," and it stuck for life.

Around this time, Adams and his sister, Luvenia, moved out of their uncle's crowded apartment and into an apartment of their own, which Adams paid for. They didn't go far, taking a place just north of Johns Hopkins Hospital so Adams could remain close to his East Baltimore clientele. But Adams and his sister wouldn't rent for much longer. When Luvenia married, Adams bought his first home and shared it with his sister and brother-in-law before ultimately giving it to them. The house purchase aside, Adams was doing all he could to conserve cash. He needed it for the next bold phase of his expansion.

Having hired more sub-writers, Adams quietly began to withhold bets from his numbers banker, brashly performing that function himself. The risks were numerous and potentially devastating. If his boss discovered the gambit, he could have easily put an end to Adams's business, and potentially more. Moreover, serving as a banker required Adams to save and account for his money with great care. If Adams couldn't pay off all of his winners, he would be exposed. Players would be furious and word would certainly get to the bank with which they thought they were ultimately doing business. Adams couldn't really protect himself as other smaller numbers bankers did by laying off bets. Laying off was a form of insurance for bankers to spread the risk when wagering was particularly heavy on a specific number or numbers. For example, if a large number of bettors placed their money on, say, 123, a hit of 123 could deplete the banker's resources. To shield himself, the banker could turn some of those wagers over — laying them off — to another banker. Adams couldn't avail himself of this maneuver. There was simply no one who possessed the two attributes he had to have: his trust and more capital than he had. So on occasions when betting was heavy on a given number, he took an alternative route, having one of his employees play the same number with another banker. But that didn't protect him from the historic development about to grip Maryland and the nation.

As the U.S. economy continued to deteriorate in the early 1930s, with unemployment surging to 25 percent and the stock market plunging 75 percent from its 1929 high, the rate of bank failures soared. From 1930 to 1933, roughly one out of every three banks collapsed. Because deposits were not yet insured by the federal government, customers of these shuttered institutions lost an estimated $140 billion — more than $2 trillion in today's dollars. Seeing their family, friends, and neighbors completely wiped out through no fault of their own, customers of surviving banks rushed to demand the return of their deposits, which resulted in still more bank failures. Hope, however, was on the horizon. President Herbert Hoover, whom many blamed for the worsening Depression, had been trounced in his November 1932 re-election bid. The victor, Franklin Delano Roosevelt, won by convincing Americans that he could put the country back to work. But many worried that better times would come too late. At the time, presidents weren't sworn in until March, four months after the election. With the economy unraveling by the day, if not the hour, Maryland Gov. Albert C. Ritchie decided his state couldn't hold on until Roosevelt took the oath of office. On February 24, 1933, Ritchie issued an executive order, shutting down all of the state's banks for three days. The so-called holiday would give otherwise healthy institutions the temporary reprieve they needed to recover from the run on their deposits. Shortly after taking office, President Roosevelt followed Ritchie's lead, declaring a four-day federal bank holiday. What was good for banks was not necessarily good for depositors, and this was particularly so for William Adams. Unexpectedly cut off from his savings, Adams didn't have sufficient funds to pay off all of his winners. His gig appeared to be up. Once the established numbers bankers discovered his covert activities, they would certainly push him out forever. He wouldn't even be able to get so much as a runner's job after this. Two years of planning and working and dreaming were on the verge of being erased like the savings of so many Americans.

006 A BANKER BREAKS IN

Facing a crisis with the potential to decimate his fledgling operation, Adams had to act fast. Winning bettors would need to be paid within a matter of hours or his ruse would be up. If Little Willie or one his staffers didn't deliver on time, players would grow suspicious. If they didn't deliver that day at all, hell would break loose. Delinquent runners frequently found themselves targets of vigilante manhunts. People loved Little Willie for his reliability. But if he failed to deliver, even just this once, the love and fealty would likely devolve into ire and spur defections.

Fortunately for him, Adams devised a solution in time. He found an individual willing to float him the necessary cash in exchange for an ongoing partnership. Adams never revealed the person's identity, for that would have put the partner at risk of retribution from established bankers. Two possible candidates were men who would be life-long friends and business partners of Adams: Irvin Kovens or Maurice L. Lipman, an individual who would go on to literally save Adams's life.

Regardless, after the scare, Adams modified his expansion plans, deciding to reduce his financial exposure while waiting out the economic volatility shaking the nation in such uncertain and unpredictable ways. He quietly resumed a greater reliance on his white banker. The patient man, he concluded, would live to see better days.

While he lived and worked on the east side, Adams made frequent trips to the all-black section on Baltimore's west side. Though just a few miles away, the two communities were worlds apart culturally. The west side, which came to be known as the Gold Coast, was where Negroes with educations and white-collar jobs tended to live. The east side, meanwhile, was home to a concentration of uneducated black laborers. There was a social structure, a hierarchy, and those with educations stood at the top. A real rivalry emerged between the two sides of the city, sometimes resulting in fights. Young men, for example, would protect their neighborhood girls from suitors residing on the other side. Nevertheless, the west side proved too alluring for many east siders to resist, for it was also home to Pennsylvania Avenue, which was rapidly becoming one of the premier places in the world for black entertainment. Ella Fitzgerald, Fats Waller, and Billie Holiday all performed on The Avenue.

Taking a break from work one evening, Adams and Kenneth Bass, an Adams sub-writer and an increasingly close friend, made their way to a west side diner to eat. Victorine Quille, a 21-year-old teacher who lived only blocks away, also patronized the establishment that evening. She hadn't really planned on being there. She was on a date.

After taking in a movie at the nearby Harlem Theater, her companion scrambled to keep the evening going. He proposed a walk or a cab ride or a sandwich. Anything. Victorine chose to walk to the restaurant for a quick bite. She needed — and wanted — to get home soon. Her first-grade students needed her to be fresh, and her parents needed her financial contribution. As a teacher, Victorine ranked among the most highly compensated Negroes in the city, earning $130 month. She had started out making $100, but after successfully completing a year in the classroom, she had been "made," the term then used for what was effectively tenure. By contrast, her father's monthly income had been slashed from $100 to $48 when the Depression worsened. A truck driver, Joseph C. Quille supplemented his earnings by moonlighting as a chauffeur to a man who understood his vices well. Both a hard-core gambler and a hard-core drinker, he recognized he needed a little help to stay in the game, which was good for the Quilles. By combining his income with that of his wife, Estelle, a hairdresser and waitress, and Victorine, the family was able to afford to remain in Baltimore's most prestigious black neighborhood, Sugar Hill.

Although Victorine was eager to leave the diner and return home that night, she didn't do so before being introduced to Adams by a mutual acquaintance. Inherently taciturn, Adams didn't say much, but he made enough of an impression to convince her to overlook the east side-west side divide and agree to go out on a date. Their first outing consisted of a ride in Adams's Ford. Victorine immediately appreciated how neat, quiet, and unassuming he was. What Adams did have to say centered on education and empowerment. He admired the fact that Victorine was a high-school graduate, well read, and a teacher. He confided that he felt ill-equipped to become a better business man because he had so little education himself. In fact, he had the same concern for many of the Negroes he knew and encountered throughout the city. In the late 1920s, the high school graduation rate in the mid-Atlantic states stood at just 20 percent. During the next decade, it nearly tripled to roughly 60 percent.

Too many knew too little, he believed, and that fact was much more than a lamentable shame. He was convinced that the way for Negroes to escape poverty and mitigate, or even eliminate, segregation was through business, through blacks creating and operating successful businesses of all types. But success would remain inaccessible and unattainable so long as blacks were undereducated, he thought. The statistics supported Adams. In 1935, Baltimore was home to the nation's fifth largest black population, 142,106 people. But in terms of black-owned businesses, the city ranked much lower. For instance, while Baltimore boasted 383 black-owned retail stores, 36 percent more than in 1929, it trailed Detroit, home to the country's seventh largest Negro community, by a gaping margin: 121 stores. What's more, all of Baltimore's black retailers combined employed just 640 people — less than two per store on average. A group called the Association for the Promotion of Negro Business conducted an economic analysis and found that blacks spent less than 2 cents out of every dollar with black businesses.

With relatively few Negro entrepreneurs to observe

and emulate, Adams closely monitored the business practices and habits of white store owners, particularly those who were Jewish. He marveled at how so many of them immigrated to the United States with nothing and yet were able to build flourishing businesses. Like him, they demonstrated unfailing discipline. They seemed to save what little they had and invest it to build something bigger and stronger. Adams forged so many relationships with Jewish businesspeople that others started derisively referring to him as a "Jew boy." The name-calling didn't bother him a bit.

While William and Victorine hit it off right away, not everyone in the Quille household possessed enthusiasm for Adams. Victorine's mother was fond of Adams from the start. Her father, well acquainted with gamblers and hustlers, wavered. Like most of black Baltimore, Victorine knew about Adams's involvement in the numbers, but she didn't really understand his business. Victorine's own mother played. A man would visit their house. Estelle and the writer would sit down at the table, and she would bet a penny on the number. "I knew ... if you hit, the man brought you money," she recalled years later. "If you hit and he didn't bring you money, then he was in trouble. Everybody would say, 'don't play with him because he doesn't pay off.'" Victorine didn't press Adams for more information, and he certainly didn't volunteer any.

Despite the reservations of Victorine's father, William, during a subsequent ride in his car, proposed marriage and Victorine accepted. On July 28, 1935, the couple married at St. Peter Claver Church in West Baltimore He was 21; she 23.

Less than six months later, with an assist from Baltimore City's top prosecutor and two criminal court judges, Adams took another big step in his life. On the final day of 1935, Baltimore State's Attorney J. Bernard Wells and the judges launched an investigation into the city's underworld racket, and they did so independent of the police department, convinced that dirty cops were making the illegal gambling possible. A spate of violence served as the catalyst. The prosecutor and judges attributed the attacks to dissent among the competing syndicates. There were now 19 such organizations in Baltimore fighting for a share of the $5 million-a-year business, according to estimates. Within two days, every known syndicate suspended operations, waiting to see how far Wells would go. Several prominent numbers men went a step further, skipping town. It didn't take investigators long to learn how the gambling outfits were operating unmolested by law enforcement. All of the big shops contributed five percent of their proceeds to a fund used to purchase police protection.

The State's Attorney publicly criticized the police department for refusing to cooperate with the massive undertaking. In all, some 1,000 people were interviewed. Dozens of underworld figures were indicted, including George Goldberg, the head of Six & Eight where Adams got his start in the business. The grand jury also accused 22 police officers of taking part in the numbers. James M. Hepbron, the managing director of a civilian criminal justice organization, prophetically summarized the situation: If police and prosecutors fail to extirpate the numbers, organized crime will "blossom."

For Adams, the disruption represented an opportunity. He'd been planning for some time to establish a numbers operation of his own, and suddenly the field was all but clear of competitors, at least temporarily. He was untroubled about becoming ensnared in the ongoing investigation, believing that the legal establishment cared little, if at all, about what transpired in the black community. "Back then, whites almost never came into the black community," Adams said years later. "So the police didn't know where to look for me. The community hid me from them, that's why I wasn't indicted with the rest. I learned how to survive outside of the law. I moved from house to house, working out of one kitchen one day and another the next."

Just as important, if not more so, he was ready to make his final daring move. Always a miser, he had saved enough money. A careful and thoughtful manager, he had built an organization strong enough to sustain success. As reliable as sunrise, he had earned the loyalty of a substantial customer base. And the U.S. economy, at very long last, appeared to be on its way to recovery. The country's gross domestic product, a broad measure of economic output, had increased an astounding 34 percent since 1932. The unemployment rate, meanwhile, had been halved. No more working for a white banker. Little Willie was going independent. He was going to be a banker himself. A kingpin. So monumental was the initiative that Adams broke with habit and actually shared the news with his wife. One evening he turned to her and declared: I am a banker. Victorine laughed dismissively. She didn't know much about the numbers, but she, like every other Negro in town, knew that there was no such thing as a black banker. Blacks didn't have enough money or clout to take on the white underworld. Not even Tom Smith, the most powerful colored man in town, could operate independently. But it's true, William assured Victorine. Improbably enough, it remained true and without incident until June 13, 1938.

Until the explosion.

007 INVESTIGATION LAUNCHED

The blast shook Adams's building with sufficient ferocity to fling three women from their beds on the second floor and to nearly claim the life of a Baltimore City police officer doing foot patrol in the neighborhood. "I was walking up the alley in the rear of the tavern and just before I reached the Whitelock Street side of the building, there was a flash and a terrific blast," Officer John Lee told a reporter. "The force of the explosion shook through me like an electric shock and I was forced a few steps backward by what felt like a pressure of wind." Immediately thereafter, shards of glass from blown-out windows rained down on the street. "If I had been a few seconds sooner, I would have reached the tavern door to try the knob just as the explosion would have happened. It was the worst experience I have ever had, and it will be a long time before I stop remembering how narrow my escape was."

For his part, Adams scrambled down the stairs to see what was going on. The street outside his nightclub was shrouded in smoke. As it cleared, Adams saw the devastation all around him. Up and down the block, windows were missing. Brick walls on both sides of the street were scarred and pocked by shrapnel. Investigators would later find a two-inch piece of pipe embedded in the exterior brick wall of a neighboring home. Although Adams had invested heavily on the nicest materials available, the doors and windows of his nightclub were blown into non-existence. Inside, the walls and ceilings were shredded. It appeared that the explosion went off in the doorway leading into Little Willie's Inn. Miraculously, no one suffered serious physical injury. Emotional injuries were another story. A shaken neighbor, James Prattis, said the explosion was another sign that he and his family were jinxed. Upstairs, Victorine was so upset that she took a rare day off of work on Monday to rest and recuperate. "I was very tired and almost asleep when the bed on which I was lying shook so much I thought it was an earthquake," Victorine recalled later during a newspaper interview. "I was so terrified I did not know what had happened until sometime later when my husband came back and told me there was an explosion."

Even before the smoke cleared, the police, thanks to a serendipitous break, had a strong lead in the case. The explosion, they believed, was no accident. On routine patrol near Little Willie's Inn 25 minutes before the blast, Sergeant Wilbur Martindale and Patrolman Edgar F. Wilson spotted a car pulling away from the curb with its headlights off. The driver then sped through a stop sign. The officers tailed the car for about a mile before pulling it over. Oddly enough, the driver's only passenger sat directly behind him in the back seat rather than next to him in the front seat. Odd, but not illegal. They issued a ticket to the driver and went on their way. But when they learned of the explosion, their minds turned immediately to the driver and his passenger, and not just because of the traffic violation.

Just one day earlier, there had been a bomb attack in another Baltimore neighborhood. Eyewitnesses told police that the bomb had been thrown from a moving car, with one of the occupants yelling out that the intended target was someone who had failed to make a payment. All of the witnesses reported that they were unable to discern the target's name. Or perhaps they eyewitnesses chose not to disclose this bit of information for fear of reprisal. Regardless, the explosion at Little Willie's Inn looked suspiciously similar.

There were many possible reasons someone would have wanted to harm or even kill Adams in the summer of 1938. For one, he was siphoning money away from white gambling operators, who were back in business following the 1936 investigation, and from white tavern owners. A white proprietor frustrated by his inability to compete legally with Adams could have launched such an attack without much, if any, risk of arrest or prosecution.

Another possibility had to do with the role he was playing to advance civil rights. Lillie Mae Jackson, who would come to be known as the mother of civil rights, was leading an effort to challenge the discriminatory practices of Baltimore's clothing retailers. The situation was execrable. Some stores barred Negroes altogether. Some permitted blacks to come in and purchase clothing, but prohibited them from trying on items before making a purchase. After all, what if a Negro tried on a garment and decided not to buy it? The store would get stuck with the item unless another Negro bought it because no white customer would purchase something worn by a colored person, even if for just one minute. As if that weren't enough, white shop owners who relied heavily on black patronage would not hire black employees. Jackson wanted dramatic change, and she had the law at her back. On March 28, 1938, the Supreme Court of the United States ruled in *New Negro Alliance et al v. Grocery Co. Inc.* that people could legally picket stores for refusing to hire colored workers. What Jackson didn't have on her side was capital. Such campaigns cost money, but the black community simply didn't have much to spare. One of the only sources of significant cash was Adams. When Jackson turned to him for help, he happily delivered. Of course, there were many people who wanted to thwart the drive. Thugs had physically assaulted picketers in previous campaigns, including Thurgood Marshall's wife. It wasn't much of a stretch to theorize that an opponent would have looked to intimidate or eliminate the source of financing. If opponents were successful in derailing the protests, the black community couldn't count on support from their local lawmakers. When asked about his views regarding the retailers' discriminatory practices, Baltimore City Councilman Meyer Reamer expressed outright surprise, as if he had never heard of it, despite the fact that he represented the city's fourth district where Negroes outnumbered whites two to one. He called the policy "un-American." Blacks and whites should intermingle in business, he said. However, he added, the races should be kept separate in theaters and places of amusement.

Still another possibility for the assault on Adams:

someone wanted to force him into paying protection money for his nightclub, a common gangster practice. There were many plausible explanations, but only Adams and those behind the bombing knew the truth, and it was in nobody's interests — not even Adams's — to share that information with the authorities.

But police didn't need a motive at that point. They had a suspect: the driver who left the site of the attack only minutes before the explosion, along with his passenger, a man possessing "maroon eyes," according to police. Better yet, they had the driver's home address as a result of the traffic ticket. Police arrested him before sunrise and took him to police headquarters for interrogation. The passenger, however, couldn't be found. The press did report that "a mystery car bearing Pennsylvania license plates was seen speeding" out of the city headed north. "In some manner the car escaped."

That afternoon, police brought their suspect before Magistrate Harry W. Allers for an initial hearing. As the victim, Adams was required to attend the proceeding and stand less than five feet away from the man suspected of trying to kill him and his wife. Although Adams hadn't seen who bombed his business and home, he recognized his alleged attacker, Julius Fink. A self-described produce vendor, Fink went by the nickname Blinky, an appellation he picked up in childhood as a result of his propensity for blinking excessively. Adams told police he had seen Fink milling around town for a number of years but that the two men were still less than acquaintances. However, Adams continued, Fink and another man had tried to forge a new relationship with him a couple of weeks earlier. As Adams stood on a sidewalk talking with a friend, Fink pulled his car up and introduced Adams to his passenger, a man Fink referred to only as "Willie." "Willie" had instructions for Adams. "We're coming into town," the man said, according to Adams. "We've been around and know everybody in the business. They've all got to give five percent. That means you, too. There won't be any meetings and no talking. We'll give you our phone number. We start on Monday." Adams told police he was confused by the demand. A percentage of what? His whiskey business? The man said yes, Adams told police. As the men drove away, Adams noted that the car had a Pennsylvania license plate.

Just as "Willie" promised, they did start the following week. Fink ducked into Little Willie's Inn looking for Adams and his payment. Failing to find him, Fink left a note, demanding an immediate phone call. The club's manager took the note and slipped it into the cash register. But he forgot to mention it to Adams, who didn't learn of the note until after the bombing. Regardless, Adams had no intention of cooperating. Exactly one week after the "start date," the explosion took place.

As was customary, the presiding magistrate called on the police to present their evidence against Fink immediately. But police pleaded for more time. Fink had a passenger when police pulled him over. And that individual — a serious suspect in what appeared to be a growing campaign of mobster violence — remained at large. If they disclosed their case at this point and if Fink were released on bail, their investigation would be badly compromised, if not ruined. "We have reason to believe that the same people did both jobs," Detective Lieutenant William

Feehley said, referring to the two bombings on successive nights. Fink's "freedom will jeopardize our investigation, we believe," Feehley added.

Through his lawyer, Fink denied any involvement in the bombing. But the plea of innocence failed to secure his release. Roughly 12 hours after the bombing, prosecutors formally charged Fink, age 42, with "assault with intent to murder one William Adams, Negro, by placing a bomb on premises at 2340 Druid Hill avenue." Allers granted the request for a postponement, giving the police two more full days — Tuesday and Wednesday — to complete their work. He also ordered that that Fink be held at the Northern Police Station rather than at the central city jail, a move that touched off rumors that authorities were concerned Fink would be murdered in central by mobsters afraid that he would start naming names in exchange for his release. Fink's next hearing was set for Thursday morning. The pressure was on the police, and the magistrate wouldn't be the only one to apply it.

008 MOB INVASION

On Tuesday, June 14, 1938, the morning newspaper broke the chilling news to the public at large: "Bomb terrorism, similar to that used by big-time racketeers in other cities, apparently has invaded Baltimore, it was feared last night by police." The two weekend explosions weren't accidents or isolated incidents. They appeared to be well-planned attacks executed by the nation's most fearsome gangsters, and the worst, in all likelihood, was yet to come. The headline in *The Sun* newspaper blared the baleful news: Baltimore, it seemed, was about to plunge down the same bloody path as New York and Chicago, blazed by merciless thugs armed with weapons and memorable nicknames such as Lucky and Bugsy. To make matters even worse, there were those in the city who were deeply concerned that the Baltimore City Police Department couldn't be trusted to conduct a thorough and honest investigation, that the force was rife with corruption. How else to explain the fact that illegal gambling operators such as Adams were never arrested? It's

51

not as if their activities were conducted in secret. In fact, they collected and paid off bets on street corners and sidewalks throughout the city, sometimes directly in front of police precincts.

Within hours of the second bombing, Police Commissioner William L. Lawson and Baltimore Mayor Howard Jackson held an emergency meeting to discuss the crimes and formulate a plan of action. Afterward, Lawson announced that every available officer would be reassigned to the investigation. At this early stage, the police hypothesized that the second bomb was intended to intimidate Adams into paying a "tribute" to out-of-town racketeers, the tribute being a percentage of his nightclub business. This was consistent with what Adams had told them. Lawson assigned John Cooney, among others, to take leadership of the investigation. It was a natural choice. Cooney was the city's top detective. But his selection spurred an already wary group of prominent citizens into action.

John Cooney and his brother Michael, who was also a city police officer, had recently been subjected to an internal investigation for allegedly taking gifts from a suspected illegal gambling boss. Without any explanation, the investigation had been indefinitely postponed. The public was told nothing about whether they'd been cleared or otherwise. That had been bad enough. But citizens concerned about the future of Baltimore were not going to let John Cooney play a pivotal role in the most important investigation in modern city history. They may have been willing to look the other way when crime remained confined to one of the city's four all-black neighborhoods.

But now that big-time gangsters were invading and potentially threatening the peace in white neighborhoods, the time for silence and complacency was over. In a private letter, the group called on Lawson to remove both of the Cooney brothers from the bombing cases and to launch an independent investigation into police corruption. Lawson was not receptive.

Meanwhile, the investigation appeared to be moving forward. A preliminary review of bomb fragments strongly suggested the two attacks were related. Police also had discovered the identity of the man who owned the car Fink drove the night of the attack. They had tracked the vehicle's Pennsylvania license plate number to a Philadelphia resident. At the behest of authorities in Baltimore, Philadelphia police apprehended the registered owner and seized his car. In doing so, they found something more, something worse, something that gave Baltimore and its residents — particularly Adams — reason to be very afraid, if they weren't already.

The suspected get-away car was also connected to a grisly triple homicide executed just one day after the Baltimore bombing. The three victims, their bodies ravaged by machine-gun fire, had been discovered in a deserted building, a former tavern, just outside Philadelphia in the town of Tamaqua. All three men were well-known numbers operators. Police suspected they were murdered for refusing to pay a percentage of their gambling business to a Philadelphia criminal boss. The press described the murders as a "gangland slaying." The theory that the violence was only just beginning in Baltimore immediately picked up ghastly momentum.

Baltimore police raced to Philadelphia to question the car's owner. The vehicle was registered under the name James Santore. But the name and address were falsified. The owner's real name was William Santore. The discovery was critical. The names now matched. Adams said the man who demanded payments was introduced to him as "Willie." After interrogating him in Philadelphia for several hours, Baltimore police returned home with Santore in their custody at 1:30 a.m. on Thursday morning. But he wouldn't stay for long. Santore, 27, convinced police that he wasn't involved in the Baltimore bombings. Santore worked as a laborer with the Works Progress Administration, a federal jobs program created by President Roosevelt. But the interview did yield some useful information. Santore didn't own the car outright. He shared ownership with another man who had been using it almost exclusively in recent weeks. But the new lead was a dead end. Santore's co-owner was one of the three men gunned down outside Philadelphia.

Despite the setbacks, the case against Fink proceeded later that Thursday, as scheduled. Adams again stood within an arm's length of the man accused of trying to kill him. The men were a study in contrasts. Two inches shy of six feet tall, lean at roughly 155 pounds, and exhibiting military-grade posture, Adams, 24, wore a conservative business suit and tie, as well as an expression of cool defiance. Fink, 42, a squat tree stump of a man, wore an open-collar, short-sleeve shirt and a bulbous pinky ring. Adams was the only Negro in the room overcrowded with police, lawyers, and reporters. As he had three days earlier, Adams positively identified Fink as one of the two men who had stopped him on the street and demanded a percentage of his alcohol revenue. But this time, the authorities challenged Adams's story. Weren't Fink and his accomplice really after a piece of the gambling racket that Adams allegedly operated? Adams adamantly denied the theory, saying he had no connection to gambling. If there were any doubts about the veracity of Adams's story, authorities concluded that they could wait. The magistrate set Fink's bail at $10,000 and turned the case over to the grand jury.

The results of the hearing in no way mollified the ad hoc group of concerned citizens. To their thinking, the fact remained: Corrupt cops could not be counted on to lead an investigation that might turn off the spigot of bribe money. The group's leaders weren't uninformed reactionaries. They were members of the Baltimore Criminal Justice Commission, a private group founded in response to a rash of crimes in 1922. Their stated mission was to examine and improve the administration of criminal justice "through constructive and helpful cooperation."

Their goal may have been cooperation with law enforcement, but the police department's commissioner appeared uninterested in reciprocating. Unable to reach Commissioner Lawson by telephone phone on Thursday, the group's leaders staked out his home in the early morning hours of Friday, June 17. They crowded onto the commissioner's front porch to await his return from work. The group's unofficial leader and spokesperson, Marie Bauernschmidt, a woman who came to be known as "The Carrie Nation of Baltimore" for her crusading, high-volume activism, reiterated their demands when he finally arrived. Replace the Cooneys and set up a special investigation into alleged police involvement with illegal gambling leaders or else. Mrs. Bauernschmidt had already demonstrated that she was someone to be reckoned with. In the past, she had taken to the radio airwaves to call for reform. And more recently, her figurative fingerprints were all over a highly inflammatory leak to the press. An unnamed source briefed *The Sun* newspaper about confidential information Bauernschmidt's group had provided to Commissioner Lawson to convince him to remove the Cooneys and launch an independent investigation. "This information," *The Sun* reported, "is said to have linked together in the crime world, in the order of their importance, lawyers with important political connections and strong underworld hookups; figures in the political world; members of the police force and underworld gangsters." Although unsubstantiated, the allegation possessed the air of plausibility based on the events of recent years. Two years earlier, for instance, more than 20 police officers had been indicted for conspiracy to violate lottery laws. Consequently, the leak worked to perfection. Alarmed by the claims, other prominent leaders from the business and legal communities joined the citizens' group in calling for changes at the police department. Baltimore, it seemed, was trapped between invading mobsters and corrupt cops.

By Friday, June 17, the police investigation into the bombings was clearly faltering. They couldn't identify the person with Fink the night of the attack, and they couldn't locate the car he had driven. Since they'd concluded Santore's car wasn't the one used in the bombing, despite the fact that the license plate numbers matched, Baltimore police initiated a new search. For their part, Philadelphia police promised a solution to the triple homicide within a matter of hours, which might, with any luck, produce the other at-large suspect in the Adams bombing case, or at least someone with knowledge of the attack.

Baltimore police had made one important advance, determining that the two weekend bombings were unrelated. The first stemmed from a labor dispute centering on the construction of a water tunnel under the city. Within a matter of days of this breakthrough, a bomb blast at the actual work site would claim 10 lives, all of them Negroes, despite the fact that blacks were effectively prohibited from working without white supervision at the project. The situation in Baltimore appeared to be deteriorating quickly and dramatically. Investigators continued to search without success for the man seen with Fink the night of the bombing. Complicating matters, they were confronted by an increasingly irate public. In response, Commissioner Lawson issued a statement declaring his refusal to make personnel changes on the team investigating the bombing of Adams's property. The increasingly heated impasse and the severity of the crimes spurred Maryland's governor, Harry W. Nice, to join the fray on Saturday, June 18. "I am charging the Police Department of Baltimore City with the responsibility now to clean up the city, drive out racketeers and accomplish the arrest and conviction of those responsible for the recent bombings, who are potential murderers and whose acts have made shambles of two sections of the city," he declared in a prepared statement. He added that there would be time to "sift rumors" about the police department after the crimes were solved. The editorial cartoon in the newspaper the next day said it all.

The drawing featured two men, one giant in stature, the other much smaller. The big man is named "racketeer influences." The small man: "Baltimore Police Department." Police Commissioner Lawson's refusal to cooperate or even negotiate with the citizens' group was effectively turning unrelated bombing cases into something considerably bigger, raising the question of why. The group hadn't asked Lawson to terminate the Cooneys, just to reassign them. Had he granted their request, then they likely would have backed off, freeing police to conduct their investigations without the constant spotlight of attention. Was he afraid of what an independent investigation would turn up? Or did he just consider it unnecessary for the commissioner of the Baltimore City Police Department to accede to the wishes of private citizens? Regardless, if he thought the outrage would dissipate, he was wrong, and for that error he would soon face life-changing consequences.

009 YOUR HEAD, PLEASE

Wholly unimpressed with how the police commissioner and the governor responded to the demands of her group, Maria Bauernschmidt shared her candid assessment with anyone who would listen. After publicly calling the police commissioner "too stupid" to take her group's advice, Bauernschmidt issued the following statement to the press: "I have read Governor Nice's statement with more amusement than interest. Does he believe that the citizens have forgotten the fact that I have frequently referred in radio addresses to unsolved criminal cases that have been committed in this city?"

Bauernschmidt added an incriminating piece of evidence: The state's attorney had sought her help in the Adams bombing case because he had become convinced that he would not receive the assistance he needed from the police department. On Tuesday, June 21, eight days after the Adams bombing, the crime commission's members decided to take bolder action. They formally voted for the creation of a permanent racket squad independent of the detective bureau led by John Cooney. And they went a step further, demanding the termination of Commissioner Lawson. "The commission views with grave concern the present conditions in the Police Department and believes that a serious responsibility rests upon the governor to prevent a further decline in the morale of the department and the further loss of public confidence in it. In the judgment of the commission, no permanent improvement will take place until the resignation of the present commissioner is obtained, and a man especially qualified for this difficult post, free from any political entanglements, is appointed."

Left unsaid was the unusual career path Lawson had taken to become the city's top cop. Before his appointment, Lawson worked as a stockbroker, not a public safety official. He had also just served as a fundraiser for Governor Nice's election campaign. The power to appoint Baltimore's police commissioner had been shifted from the city's mayor to the state's governor to eliminate the possibility of a patronage appointment and ensure that the critical post would be filled by the most qualified person for the job. After the commission demanded his resignation, Lawson softened his position, offering to hold public hearings regarding claims of police corruption, a proposal the governor called "splendid."

Again, Bauernschmidt was unimpressed. Nice, she believed, would rig any allegedly independent body to find in his favor, and in this instance the stakes were entirely too high. Baltimore, she and others were convinced, was at real risk of being taken over by mobsters. Since the repeal of

Prohibition, big-city gangsters looked to Baltimore as an expansion opportunity. It was close to other big cities where they were already entrenched, and, more important, it didn't have a kingpin with homicidal tendencies. There were a bunch of smaller, unaffiliated criminals, but no major forces. New York's Dutch Schultz was one of the first, charging one of his top men to set up shop in Baltimore.

Whether Baltimore's police knew it at the time or not, Schultz had already perfected his method for taking over successful numbers rackets. In 1931, a black West Indian named Big Joe Ison dominated the numbers in Harlem, New York. As Ison stood on a street corner one day, a car pulled up and the occupants, Bo Weinberg and Abe Landau, ordered him to get in. They demanded a cut of Ison's business and gave him one week to decide whether to agree to their terms or pay other undetermined consequences. They then threw him out on the street. With nowhere to turn for protection, Ison relented. By one estimate, Schultz's operation generated $20 million in annual revenue by the close of 1932, thanks to repeat performances in cities up and down the East Coast. However, Schultz's first foray into Baltimore failed. When the federal government discovered that the man Schultz assigned to Baltimore was an illegal resident, they used the threat of deportation to get him to talk about his mob relations. He was soon murdered.

As the days passed, the mainstream white media devoted more coverage to the charges of police and political corruption and less to the case that sparked those claims: the Adams bombing case. But the city's black newspaper, the *Baltimore Afro-American*, remained focused on the investigation. On July 2, the Afro reported that police believed they were drawing close to a resolution. Their cause for optimism was the discovery that Adams misled them when he said Julius "Blinky" Fink and "Willie" wanted a piece of his whiskey business. Authorities were now certain that the bombing stemmed directly from Adams's involvement in the numbers. Armed with this knowledge, police were pursuing a new investigatory course that was generating positive results. The Baltimore Police Department dispatched detectives to seek out and question known numbers figures in Atlantic City, Philadelphia, and Washington, convinced that Blinky and Willie were working for an out-of-town racket. The *Afro* newspaper also provided some political cover to Governor Nice, who was coming under increasingly heavy fire from the city's crime commission. With Nice expected to run for re-election in four months, the newspaper declared him the "best governor Maryland ever had," explaining that he done more "to bring real democracy to colored citizens than any other governor in the history of the State." It was Nice, after all, who paved the way for the appointment of the very first Negroes to the uniformed city police department. And with Nice at the helm, the state had gone more than three years without a lynching, this at a time when whites, struggling with the Great Depression, were renewing their reliance on the rope.

One year before Nice took office in 1934, a Negro on Maryland's Eastern Shore named George Armwood had been lynched for allegedly raping an 82-year-old white woman. Not satisfied by killing the suspect before he had chance to stand trial, the white mob cut off the dead man's ear, stabbed him in the chest, and then dragged his body to the town square, where they doused it in gasoline and set it ablaze. Although the heinous attack transpired more than 100 miles away from Baltimore, the *Afro* newspaper dispatched one its cub reporters, Clarence Mitchell, to relay the horror to the city's black community. The *Afro* also came to the defense of the police commissioner, who fulfilled the governor's pledge to add black police to his department. In an editorial, the newspaper expressed concern that the white citizens' group was putting too much emphasis on the bombing cases and claims of police corruption. "The [Adams] bombing, as serious as it is, is being overworked to keep the atmosphere foggy despite the fact that there has been an arrest and the crime has been acted upon by the grand jury." What the police department really needs to focus on is prostitution, the paper's editor opined. Prostitution is rampant because of the bad economy and because it takes two to three years to secure a divorce.

In mid-July, the Baltimore City Police Department launched a city-wide campaign to crack down on all types of vice, an initiative that prompted some to wonder whether Commissioner Lawson was trying divert attention away from the stalled bombing investigations and his own mounting troubles. In one sweep, more than 30 people were arrested for numbers. Others were picked up being in possession of untaxed alcohol.

Meanwhile, during the month that followed the bombing, Adams worked hard to restore and reopen his nightclub. In the July 16 edition of the *Afro*, he let black

Baltimore know that he was ready to resume. "Everything in full swing again at Little Willie's Inn," his advertisement triumphantly declared. The Jimmie Jenkins' orchestra was to perform, and matinees were scheduled for Thursday and Sunday. For those who wanted dinner with their entertainment, Adams promised the "best seafood in season." The black community's certain excitement at regaining the popular nightspot was tempered by two pieces of disheartening news.

The Ku Klux Klan had burned a cross in front of Maryland home where a black man was living with a white woman. "This is a first warning," the KKK said in a posted notice. "We'll be back." And closer to home, on Pennsylvania Avenue, a black beautician was evicted from the store she rented because of her race, a fact the attorney for the building's owner contested. The incident touched off the *Afro's* polymathic editor, Carl Murphy Jr. "That there should be any white merchants on Pennsylvania Avenue who would object to the presence of a legitimate colored business place in their block calls for more than passing attention," he wrote. "Practically all the money which keeps merchants on Pennsylvania Avenue going comes from colored consumers. But the interesting angle was the immediate reaction to the knowledge that colored people, through an organized agency, might do something about it. If, through some organized way, the colored consumers decided all at once to divert their trade from the avenue to some other section, the street would look like an alley in Goldsmith's 'Deserted Village.' We supply its life blood."

Rallied by iconic leaders such as Murphy, Lillie Mae

Jackson, and Thurgood Marshall, Baltimore's black community closed ranks and harnessed the power they possessed. If they organized, they wouldn't have to rely exclusively on the moral claims of equality and fairness, claims that stirred too few whites. If they organized, they could threaten to redirect their dollars and votes, threats that were already beginning to effect change. In late July, the city's leading black Republican Party activist, Marse S. Callaway, formed a political argument that echoed Murphy's economic disquisition. "This is the first time in the history of Maryland that we can go to the polls and vote for a man who has done something for us instead of voting for the past performances of Abraham Lincoln," he said, referring to Governor Nice. "If any colored man or colored woman in this State raises his voice against Nice and does not work for Nice in this coming campaign for his re-election as governor, he is not an enemy to Nice and to Nice's associates on his own ticket, but an enemy to his own race and he does not believe in race progress."

010 CASE CLOSED

As Baltimore moved inexorably toward the November elections, the Adams case drifted on endlessly. Police searched every garage in Baltimore looking for the car Fink drove the night of the attack. They also called on police in other East Coast cities to be on the lookout for Fink's alleged co-conspirator, a man with maroon eyes whom they were now identifying as Max Weisenberg of Philadelphia. Balimore police were convinced Weisenberg maintained an affiliation with a big-city racket elsewhere and had, therefore, returned home to seek the shelter that only his racket — and the corrupt cops the racket bought off — could provide. In this effort, Baltimore received indirect and unexpected assistance from an ambitious New York prosecutor, Thomas Dewey.

With aspirations for higher office, perhaps even the presidency, Dewey decided to raise his public profile by pursuing New York's criminal underground, which was largely financed by numbers operations. In August of 1938,

Dewey's criminal numbers case against James J. Hines, accused of being tangled up with the infamous and merciless Dutch Shultz, made news across the country. What's more, Dewey's attempted purge of New York's numbers industry prompted police and prosecutors in other cities to crackdown, as well. In Chicago, for instance, the state's attorney chased the numbers with such vigor and efficacy that the city's kingpins, who were paying a reported $9,500 a week for protection, were thinking of abandoning the business, which was generating as much as $18 million a year. In Detroit, the police redoubled their efforts, as well, snagging, among others, John W. Roxborough, Joe Louis's co-manager and the alleged boss of a major numbers syndicate. Roxborough said he had quit the numbers when out-of-town white gangsters invaded his market. A newspaper article reported that in Detroit "Colored writers working for the colored numbers barons, in many instances, were beaten and barred [by white gangsters] from the neighborhoods where they had been working for a number of years."

The purges in New York and elsewhere prompted a reporter from Baltimore's *Afro-American* newspaper to wonder whether displaced out-of-town gangsters were relocating to Baltimore. "No," according to an anonymous city detective. "Once in a while some of these so-called big shots slip in but they don't stay long," he said. "We don't tolerate them here."

To the white citizens' group demanding dramatic change at the city's police department, such assertions were laughable. The Cooney brothers were still leading the Adams investigation. And thanks to the tireless efforts of

Maria Bauernschmidt, Commissioner Lawson appeared largely discredited and on the verge of resigning. Bauernschmidt revealed that Lawson owned part of a whiskey manufacturer that he failed to report to the relatively new federal regulatory body, the Securities and Exchange Commission. Lawson was ultimately convicted of conspiracy in the case and sentenced to three years in jail.

"You have to handle politicians with kid gloves," Bauernschmidt once said, adding: "And you have to have a rock in your mitt."

While Baltimore's white community focused on the leadership of the police department, the black community received yet another reason to be concerned about the reliability of rank-and-file officers in the spring of 1939. Just three days after the Reverend Charles Randall and his wife, Virginia, rented and moved into a West Baltimore home, they came under attack from angry whites. With the addition of the Randalls, a formerly all-white block of homes was now occupied by four colored families, and some neighbors were clearly unhappy with the transition. On Friday night, a mob surrounded the house and threw rocks through the windows. Police responded to the incident by assigning a three-person special detail to the location to pre-empt additional attacks. But the next day, police stood by and watched as a group of white males broke into the Randalls' home and destroyed all of their possessions, going so far as to hurl broken furniture out of the windows. Not until a second unit arrived did the police intervene. Five people were arrested for the two-day assault, but just two of them were punished, drawing fines of $1 each.

Despite all of the distractions and a long, largely fruitless investigation, the police department, relying on a tip, located and arrested the man they believed to be Fink's accomplice, Max Weisberg, not Weisenberg as they originally thought, in June 1939, more than one full year after the bombing. The informant indicated Weisberg could be found in Philadelphia, information that proved accurate. When they arrived, police spied Weisberg leaving a residence and getting into a car, so they trailed him. Weisberg headed south, giving police hope that he might be headed to Baltimore, which might further implicate him. But when he stopped at a diner in Wilmington, Delaware, and ordered food, police arrested him. Without incident, police brought Weisberg to Baltimore's northern district police station for a late-afternoon arraignment. All they seemingly needed to solve the case once and for all was for Adams to positively identify Weisberg as the man who had demanded a percentage of his business. Sensing the end was finally near, police also picked up Julius "Blinky" Fink for the hearing.

Once again, law enforcement called on Adams to recount what happened the day two men pulled him over and demanded a percentage of his business.

"One of them said, 'Willie come over here.' I went to the car and ..." Adams paused and nodded at Weisberg, who was standing next to him at the bench. "But this is not the man." The deputy state's attorney urged Adams to continue his testimony, and he did. At the conclusion of the account, the presiding magistrate asked: "Was this the man?"

"No," Adams reiterated. "The man I saw was taller; he

was as tall as me." The assertion should have spurred follow-up questions. How can you be certain he was taller than you if he never exited the vehicle during your verbal exchange? Have you ever seen him standing? But such queries never came.

The prosecutor followed by stating that other witnesses also failed to identify Weisberg.

"Well," the magistrate said, "dismissed."

The Sun reported that Weisberg would be permitted to leave Baltimore with the car police had been holding for more than a year while they searched for him. Weisberg apparently never called to claim the vehicle, discovered abandoned on the street soon after the bombing, despite the fact that it was registered in his name.

The outcome prompted *Afro-American* newspaper editor John Murphy to unleash a vitriolic column in the next edition. "The prosecutor admits that he hasn't evidence enough to convict, and it would be foolish, in such circumstances, to proceed to trial. [He] is doubtless making the best of a bad situation, but that it is bad is beyond doubt." Murphy had a surfeit of evidence to support his argument. During the previous 10 years, there had been eight bomb attacks in Baltimore City, two of them targeting sitting mayors. And not one of them had resulted in a conviction. "This is a record that can hardly be viewed with satisfaction; for, no matter how valid the excuses, the fact remains that there are eight unpunished bomb outrages now on the list," Murphy concluded.

What Murphy and the public at large did not know was just how close police and prosecutors had come to solving the Adams case.

Wanting to put an end the year-long police manhunt for one of their members, Weisberg's mob organization decided to pursue a back-room deal with Adams. They contacted Adams's friend, Maurice "Mo" Lipman, to organize a meeting between the two sides. Mo's father had maintained horse stables on Caroline Street, not far from where Adams lived with his Uncle Reather. And Mo operated a bar across the street from Adams, at Lafayette Street and Pennsylvania. Nevertheless, Adams was understandably reluctant, but he relented because of his close relationship with, and deep fondness for, Lipman.

At Lipman's Park Avenue home in Baltimore City, the two sides met, face to face. The mob had offered to turn Weisberg over to the police if Adams would agree not to identify him. In exchange, the mob would never again attempt to interfere with Adams's numbers business. Adams agreed. And so, through intermediaries, the mob tipped off police about Weisberg's whereabouts. And Adams upheld his end of the bargain.

Although it would take several years, Baltimore's police were not through with Adams.

Meanwhile, as a special thank you to Adams, the mob delivered ringside tickets for the upcoming Joe Louis bout. Adams already had his own tickets, but he accepted them anyway. Rather ironically, by working with the mob, Adams did Baltimore a major favor that may have saved lives. Rather than run the risk of exposure in Baltimore following the Adams incident, the Mafia abandoned the city for good, an anonymous police source told *The Washington Post* roughly three decades later. "Nobody moved in after that," he said. "As much as anybody, Willie kept the Mafia out of the city." The source went one step further, adding that Adams "used to work pretty closely with the police years ago."

011 GOING LEGIT

In one way, the bombing and "failed" investigation actually strengthened Adams's numbers operation. The Mafia or Cosa Nostra controlled most of nation's illegal gambling outfits. While other operators had to be on constant lookout and pay for protection from big-city mobs, Adams no longer needed to be concerned about such matters, having forged a deal with his assailant's crew. Nevertheless, the attack shook Adams emotionally as well as physically, although he didn't disclose his feelings at the time. It wasn't in his nature to be so forthcoming, and it also wasn't in the best interest of his business. Adams abhorred violence. To his thinking, nothing in life warranted or justified attacks against people or property. Not even the big profits generated by the numbers. It was just business, nothing personal. If an employee or player crossed Adams, he would merely stop conducting business with that individual. He never resorted to assault, no matter how egregious the infraction.

However, many in Baltimore had a nearly devout belief that Adams relied on muscle to keep his operation running smoothly. In fact, there were those who thought Adams was becoming a dangerous gangster in his own right. The public perception, however false, served Adams well, according to one close business associate. Fear, after all, can be a powerful deterrent. But in reality, the bombing inspired fear in Adams. He worried about the safety of his family and friends. What if someone he cared about were injured or even killed for no reason other than being associated with Adams? As he had multiple times before, Adams developed a business plan, this one designed in part to lead his loved ones out of harm's way.

Adams desire to become a legitimate businessman intensified following the 1938 bombing. And so he took what he considered the natural next step to accomplishing his goal. Despite his growing success and wealth from the numbers, Adams, now in his mid-20s, sought out a formal education, enrolling in night school. He stuck with it, too, graduating from the Booker Washington Junior High School in 1940. The Baltimore *Afro-American* newspaper commemorated the commencement ceremony by publishing a picture of the graduating class of 58 people, imposing an arrow on the image that pointed to Adams so readers wouldn't miss their reason for including the photograph.

But night school didn't interrupt his daytime business pursuits. With the popularity of Pennsylvania Avenue's black nightclubs, such as the Royal Theater, soaring, Adams went to work developing his own entertainment venue on the Gold Coast. Employing the same process that he used to develop Little Willie's Inn, Adams bought two adjoining buildings, one of them home to a worn out bar called the Palm Tavern, and orchestrated a major renovation. On the second and third floors, Adams built rooms to accommodate visiting black entertainers at his club and others, rooms intended to be nicer than those at the all-black hotels. Adams also constructed an office for his burgeoning real estate business on the second floor. This way he could spend more time at the very heart of black Baltimore and keep an occasional eye on the comings and goings at his new first-floor establishment, the Club Casino.

Forever loyal to those who were loyal to him, Adams entrusted his new endeavor to the first two men he brought into his fledgling numbers business at the beginning of the 1930s: Kenneth Bass and Askew Gatewood. Adams didn't merely hire the men. Adams had little interest in building a team of employees. Instead, he preferred to establish strategic partnerships, a practice on which he relied throughout his life. Although he had no formal business education, Adams recognized both the power and the value of structuring organizations in this way. To begin with, the arrangement brought the partners' interests into near-perfect alignment. Instead of having one party motivated by profits and the other by paychecks and punching clocks, partners shared the same objective and the same rewards. Losses were generally a different story. Adams typically covered those himself.

Adams took a particular — but by no means exclusive — interest in partnering with African Americans. He wanted to help cultivate black business leaders, and his partnerships served as an effective means to that end. At the time, there were few if any opportunities for blacks to lead companies. Adams created such opportunities by not only providing the financing but also taking a hands-off approach to management, relying on his partners to operate the businesses. If partners asked for his input, Adams gave it. But otherwise, he left it to them.

Adams also believed that such partnerships produced benefits at the macroeconomic level. One, most businesses were owned and operated by whites who could and did deliver inferior products to colored patrons with competitive impunity. Black proprietors could right that wrong and offer customers the quality they deserved, and perhaps spur white competitors to follow suit. Just as important, black business ownership could help keep black dollars in black communities and be recycled rather than syphoned off by white proprietors.

Adams believed his money could generate more than healthy financial returns. It could also produce more important social progress by giving Negroes a chance at economic empowerment that would be felt and enjoyed throughout the larger community. "I was concerned about blacks having something," he would later say. What Bass and Gatewood received, what they had earned through service to Adams in the numbers, was the opportunity to run Club Casino as they saw fit, provided that they maintained high quality.

If the selection of Bass and Gatewood as partners appeared predictable, Adams's choice upstairs, at his second-floor real estate firm, looked fantastical, all but inconceivable — to blacks and whites alike. With Maurice "Mo" Lipman, a white Jewish man, Adams operated A&L

Realty. Blacks and whites were rarely, if ever, equal partners in anything, yet Adams voluntarily established a partnership with Lipman. Adams obviously didn't need a partner for financial reasons. He had sufficient resources to go it alone. What is more, blacks in Baltimore were legally barred from living in white neighborhoods, and here Adams elected entering the residential real estate business with a white guy, a white Jewish man, no less. In some quarters, black resentment for Jews ran high, fanned by the number of Jewish business owners in black neighborhoods and the perception that those proprietors were spiriting away with what little money they had. Adams had a more nuanced view. He saw what other Negroes saw: a disproportionate number of businesses in black neighborhoods were operated by Jews. Like others, Adams lamented the missed opportunity. But rather than turn bitter, he looked to emulate the successes he saw around him. In fact, he identified Jewish store owners as the best examples of business savvy and sacrifice, he later said. Generally speaking, they started off with little, living over their store, working long hours, spending within their means, and, most importantly, saving money, which they then used to buy more real estate and invest in the education of their children so they could go on to even greater success.

He admired people who made something of themselves in business, regardless of their race or creed. That Adams was friends with Lipman a half decade before Rosa Parks and Martin Luther King Jr. opened the first crack in legalized segregation with the successful bus boycott of the 1954 and 1955 was no real surprise. They had similar business interests and talents. In fact, Lipman owned and operated a bar directly across the street from Adams's Little Willie's Inn. And they shared something that few others did. Mo played a pivotal role in saving Adams's business, and perhaps even his life, from Philadelphia gangsters. To leave the realm of hoodlums, Adams earned his real estate broker's license shortly after the bombing. A&L Realty initially focused on buying residential properties and renting the units to tenants.

While Adams brought his most trusted numbers lieutenants into the Club Casino, he did not bring the numbers business, too. He kept his legal and illegal operations separate. He kept all documents associated with the numbers at one of the rowhouses he owned on the city's east side, where his players and runners were concentrated. He focused on the west side for his new real estate and entertainment endeavors. He meticulously maintained the division for two primary reasons. In East Baltimore, he had an established network of police officers to help provide protection for him and his business. He didn't have a similar network in West Baltimore, and he didn't want to build one. He also didn't want his legitimate businesses to become targets for police raids. Adams knew it was going to be difficult enough to transform his reputation from criminal kingpin to honest broker. He couldn't allow his new ventures to come under any suspicion.

Like Little Willie's Inn, Club Casino became a preferred destination for black celebrities to visit, eat, and relax after performing elsewhere in the city. Already the most prominent Negro in Baltimore, Adams saw his reputation further burnished. But even as he hobnobbed with the rich and famous, he continued to invest heavily to promote black business people and a better quality of life for the entire black community. Adams would launch and seed hundreds of businesses during the next half century, but he would value none as much as he did the Club Casino. This isn't to say that the nightclub was a big money-maker. It wasn't, and he shared what he earned with his partners.

Wanting to further diversify, Adams maintained a perpetual search for new opportunities and new partners. Self-conscious about his own lack of a formal education, Adams held college graduates in high esteem, particularly those who studied business. In 1944, Adams met a man who more than fit the bill. Together, they would make business history, creating the company that would become the first to break the color barrier on Wall Street. But their introduction and path to success proved circuitous.

Adams met Henry Green Parks Jr. on a northbound train to Boston. Adams was on the train at the behest of Joe Louis. Louis's wife, Marva, was to make her national debut as a singer at a white-owned nightclub, and Joe asked his friend to attend the performance to show support for her. Adams and his own wife, Victorine, had grown close to both Joe and Marva. Whenever the Adamses were in Chicago, for instance, they stayed in the Louis home. The Adamses reciprocated whenever the Louises visited Baltimore. As a result, Adams happily fulfilled Joe's request. However, he didn't look forward to hearing Marva sing. By most accounts, she didn't possess much vocal talent. But what she did have was one of the most famous men in the world as a husband, a man with strong contacts in the entertainment and marketing industries. One of the contacts was William B. Graham, the owner of a New York-based public relations firm. Graham had made a name for himself as a national sales representative for Pabst Blue Ribbon beer, which relied on Graham to get its beer into the growing number of black-owned bars and nightclubs. As a result, Graham established ties with scores of black establishments and owners on the East Coast, including Adams, whom he met on sales calls to Little Willie's Inn and the Club Casino. Louis and Graham established a relationship after Graham helped to convince his company to sponsor Louis, which represented a major marketing breakthrough. Until then, white-owned businesses would have considered an association with a colored person, no matter how famous, as a detriment, not a benefit. Consequently, Louis turned to Graham for help when Marva decided to make a go of it in show business. Graham agreed to serve as her manager. He assigned his PR firm associate, Henry Parks, to serve as her road manager, which is why he headed to Boston on the same train as Adams.

Parks also got his professional start at Pabst, securing a job by submitting an unsolicited proposal about how to win more black customers. During his tenure with the brewer, Pabst sponsored a radio program hosted by Groucho Marx. To attract Negro consumers, Parks suggested that Pabst should have the black entertainer Lena Horne guest star on the Marx show. Pabst executives agreed, writing a script that would have Horne play Marx's maid. Parks wisely counseled that this would be a mistake. Depict the revered Horne as a black stereotype, and Negro consumers will never consume our product, he explained. But his bosses couldn't figure out an alternative. If they had Horne portray a character that was an actual peer of Marx, then they would risk offending their loyal white customers. Parks devised a solution, proposing a skit where Marx would wander into a nightclub where Horne was performing.

Adams took an immediate interest in Parks. Not only did Parks share Adams's passion for business. He also possessed an enviable amount of knowledge, having earned a degree in business from the Ohio State University and accumulated a lot of street smarts while working for Pabst and Graham. Parks, who roomed with Olympic legend Jesse Owens in college, had everything Adams looked for in a business partner: formal training, strategic thinking, and relentlessness in pursuit of success. Others shared this assessment. One of Parks's college professors was so in impressed with him that he recommended an unusual post-graduation undertaking. With racism sure to hamper Parks's professional prospects, the professor suggested that Parks move to South America after graduation to learn enough Spanish so that he could pass for a Latino upon returning to the United States. Parks had a complexion light enough to pass, but no interest in doing so. In short order, Parks distinguished himself as a marketing genius, helping Graham to promote black businesses and open the growing black market to new products. Although he had only just met Parks, Adams extended an open offer. If his business with Marva Louis ended and he wanted to pursue new entrepreneurial ventures, all he had to do was call. Adams would move him from New York to Baltimore and put him to work.

When Marva's singing career eventually flopped, Parks

called Adams and asked if his offer still stood. It did, and Parks soon found himself living with Adams's in-laws until he could find a place of his own. Within days, his professional plate was full. Adams tasked Parks with analyzing a business idea he had for establishing a lending bank for black consumers. No other institution in Baltimore would lend significant capital to blacks, which prevented them from launching companies of their own, among other things. His intentions weren't entirely altruistic. In this, he could generate a profit while also helping his community. Adams asked Parks to investigate the idea and devise a plan. Just as Adams said he would, Parks found that racist business practices by white owners had created a lucrative opportunity, much as they had in the nightclub business. White lenders were charging black customers 3.5 percent interest monthly on loans of no more than $300, generating an annual return of 42 percent. Adams could offer bigger loans at lower interest rates and still generate a substantial profit while helping the black community. But their lending business was derailed before it got out of the station. In 1945, the federal government passed a law, capping annual interest charges on loans at 12 percent. Adams's interest in the bank fizzled. He felt confident that he could develop other businesses that would produce better results.

In the meantime, Adams had Parks join his increasingly busy real estate practice. In addition to buying rowhouses throughout the city and renting them out, Adams was building a portfolio of ground rents. In Baltimore, homes and the land on which they stood were often separate assets. So someone could own a house but not the ground underneath. The governing law was obscure, but Adams studied it and uncovered an investment opportunity. By owning the underlying ground, Adams could charge the homeowner 6 percent of the property's assessed value every six months, for an annual return of 12 percent. But this 12 percent was different than the 12 percent he could have realized in the lending business. With ground rents, if the homeowner failed to pay him, he could foreclose on the house. He could take ownership while paying only for the land, which was considerably less expensive. The cost of a single ground rent was approximately $300, while rowhomes sold for $500 to $600. In one fell swoop, Adams bought the ground rents for roughly 50 homes not far from Baltimore's Inner Harbor, near the train station at Camden Yards. Coincidentally, it would be in the Camden Yards area where Adams and Parks would turn their next big idea into a ground-breaking company. It wouldn't be much longer.

012 TEEING OFF, IN COURT

No stranger to historic bouts himself, Joe Louis also touched off one of the most important fights Adams waged on behalf of racial equality. It was well known in both black and white Baltimore that Louis and Adams were close friends. Every time Louis visited, the two were the subject of newspaper stories and photographs, the setting often being Little Willie's Inn. So when Roger H. Pippen, the sports editor of Baltimore's *News-Post* newspaper, heard a rumor in the summer of 1940 that Louis would soon be in town, he contacted Adams to check it out. Adams confirmed the tip. The two intended to golf. If you want to join us, you're welcome to do so, Adams said. Invited to spend time with the biggest superstar in all of sports, Pippen accepted. The journalist didn't need to ask where they would play. In Baltimore, Negroes were permitted to golf on only one public course: Carroll Park.

After spending the afternoon with Louis, Adams, and their playing partners, Pippen wrote a column focused, predictably, on the champ's golfing prowess. "Off the tee, Louis hits a long ball. His down swing is a little fast, but at the point of contact he really explodes some power. He made several drives of 250 yards and straight down the middle. He also pulled three out of bounds. His long irons are good, too. His approaches from within eighty yards are his chief weakness," Pippen wrote. To anyone but devoted fans of Louis, the column likely held little interest, at least not until Pippen got around to evaluating Louis's putting. "As a putter, he is above average. He sank several of ten feet on the sand greens at Carroll. And that, in case you have never played there, is a feat."

Pippen, a white journalist who had been to Baltimore's other public courses, had never seen putting "greens" made of sand rather than meticulously cropped grass. Appalled by the qualitative disparity between the public courses for whites and the single course for Negroes, Pippen called on the city to close the gap. "Incidentally, with golf growing in leaps and bounds among colored people of this section, the Park Board should build grass greens at Carroll. A few traps here and there would help, too," he wrote.

News of the disparity was something of a revelation to Adams. Prohibited from playing other courses owned and operated by the city government, he didn't know that the white public facilities in Baltimore boasted grass greens. He had played on grass greens elsewhere in the country. But Adams assumed that if one public course in Baltimore had sand greens, then they all did, consistent with the governing doctrine of separate but equal. Unwilling to wait and see if the government responded to Pippen's recommendation, Adams sprang into action. The separate-but-equal law was offensive enough. But for the government to blatantly disregard even that low standard was intolerable. Adams — joined by Arnett Murphy, the vice president of the *Afro-American* newspaper, and William B. Dixon, the successful owner of a black insurance company — decided to initiate a legal fight. This wasn't just about golf. If they could create a legal fissure in the separate-but-equal doctrine, then perhaps other government institutions, such as the public school system, would be forced to provide better facilities for Negroes. The government could equivocate about how black and white schools were effectively equal. But could the city litigate its way out of the obvious difference between sand and grass?

Looking for legal representation with experience in fighting for greater racial equality, Adams, Dixon, and Murphy contacted the National Association for the Advancement of Colored People. While the NAACP and its legal team were headquartered in New York, they liked to wage legal fights in Maryland. As the northern-most southern state in the nation, Maryland presented lots of discriminatory policies to challenge. But more importantly, the state was culturally more northern. Judges and juries in Maryland were more likely to be sympathetic to their arguments than their peers in the deeper South. It was for this reason, for instance, that the NAAP brought its national fight in Maryland to open public colleges and universities to Negroes. In December 1935, Donald Gaines Murray applied to the University of Maryland School of Law at the behest of Thurgood Marshall, the NAACP's No. 2 lawyer who himself had been denied admission to his hometown law school. As Marshall expected, Maryland rejected Murray. The school helpfully suggested that Murray should apply to the Princess Anne Academy in Southern Maryland if he wished to earn a law degree, never mind the fact that the Academy didn't offer legal instruction of any kind. In the spring of 1935, the NAACP's No. 1 lawyer, the legendary Charles Houston, who had led Howard University's law school to national prominence, filed suit on Murray's behalf. Houston believed Murray's case represented a "springboard for extending the attacks [against racial segregation in the United States] on a larger front." Murray and the NAACP won the case later the same year, creating the legal precedent to fuel cases in less hospitable southern courts.

Despite the NAACP's penchant for litigating in Maryland, the organization turned down Adams and his allies. The rejection didn't stem from a lack of interest or importance. Neither was it a lack of resources, although the NAACP was operating on a shoestring budget. The president of the Baltimore chapter, Lillie M. Jackson, declined the request, explaining, Adams recalled years later with a laugh: "Well, if you fellows are wealthy enough to play golf together ... you're wealthy enough to pay your lawyers yourself." Somewhat ironically, the NAACP's financial struggles actually ended up benefitting Adams's case. In addition to a rejection, the NAACP gave Adams a reference: Charles Houston. Houston, the man who established the NAACP's pioneering legal unit, had recently made the heart-wrenching decision to leave the organization. While deeply committed to the mission of social activism, he decided he could no longer live on his meager NAACP salary and therefore left to go into private practice. In 1938, two lawyers who worked on the Donald Murray case with Marshall and Houston, Dallas Nicholas and William I. Gosnell, brought a lawsuit. Houston later joined the effort. Adams, Dixon, and Murphy paid their legal team $2,500, $100 more than Thurgood Marshall earned during his entire first year of work at the NAACP in 1936.

To make his case against the city, Houston tapped one of the nation's leading black golfers, Samuel Stewart, to testify. Stewart had won numerous championships throughout the country, including the Joe Louis tournament in Detroit. Of course, there were no big checks for black champions at the time, so Stewart had to maintain a day job, which he did as a teacher at Dunbar High School in East Baltimore for 38 years. Stewart and Adams were dear friends. Adams regularly went to Sam's house for breakfast, where fish, grits, and tomatoes were staples. And they played hundreds of rounds of golf together. When asked to reflect on the golf course litigation 40-some years later, Stewart immediately recalled one of Houston's wittier rebuttals. The city argued that courses for blacks and whites were qualitatively equal, so the two races could be kept segregated without offending the Constitution. We are willing to accept this argument, provided that the two races swap their designated courses, Houston responded. The whites could have Carroll Park if the blacks in return received Mt. Pleasant, a course so well appointed and maintained that the Professional Golf Association selected it to host professional tournaments. In fact, the great Arnold Palmer pulled off the second win of his career there in 1956.

Led by one of the nation's most formidable lawyers, Adams and his collaborators made history, becoming the first people in the country to sue a governmental entity for failing to provide qualitatively equal public recreational facilities. The potential implications were monumental. Municipalities throughout the country maintained segregated and decidedly unequal swimming pools, tennis courts, and golf courses. A victory would create the powerful legal precedent to successfully litigate elsewhere. Not surprisingly, the case also proved monumentally challenging to all involved. Positive rulings were followed by appeals and reversals. The case made it all the way to the state's highest court, the Court of Appeals, where a panel of judges upheld a demeaning compromise. Negroes would be given access to white courses, but only on Tuesdays, Wednesdays and Thursdays. On each of those days, one white course would be colored only. The days were selected because they were least popular among golfers of all colors. Despite the limited scope of the ruling, it inspired some whites to protest. Why couldn't they play on the designated Negro days, they asked? Wasn't that discriminatory? The questioning produced results. The policy was modified to permit white golfers.

The gains, modest though they were, didn't stand for long. Shortly after the end of World War II, Baltimore employed technological improvements in irrigation to convert the putting greens at the city's colored course, Carroll Park, from sand to grass. Reasoning that the Negro course was now equal to the white courses, the city reinstated segregation seven days a week. While it was true that the courses were more alike in terms of the putting greens, one significant disparity remained. Carroll Park included only nine holes. The white courses offered the 18 holes necessary for a full round.

When viewed in isolation, the litigation triggered by Adams and Louis appeared to have made little difference. Negroes received a concession that was offensively inadequate, inconvenient, and ultimately transient. But when viewed in context of the broader sweep of history, it is clear that Adams, Dixon, and Murphy, along with their lawyer, Charles Houston, opened a new front in the overarching campaign for racial equality. Their effort inspired and informed similar lawsuits throughout the country, from Miami to Denver, New Orleans to Detroit, and one of those subsequent suits made it to the Supreme Court of the United States, which in 1955 created national precedent by desegregating Atlanta's public courses.

The legal battle did nothing to dampen Adams's rabid enthusiasm for golf, which had been building steadily since his inauspicious introduction to the game. In 1937, a regular customer came into Little Willie's Inn toting a putter, a golf ball, and a sales pitch. Hoping to convince Adams to buy his clubs, the patron put on a demonstration right there on the floor of the dining room. After taking a few shots himself, Adams agreed, paying $3 for the entire set. Not until he got to Carroll Park for the first time did Adams realize his mistake. The seller had only shown him the putter, which could be used by both left-handers and right-handers. The other clubs, however, were for right-handers. The seller knew Adams was left handed, and sold them to him as a joke. The seller and Adams laughed about the story for more than a decade. But once Adams purchased the correct equipment, the laughter stopped. While Adams always preferred to spend his time working rather than playing, he did make time for golf, although it could hardly be classified as play. As usual, he wasn't interested in modest success. If it was worth playing, it was worth winning. In 1945, wanting to do more than improve his game at the margins, Adams, working with one of the nation's leading black golfers, Clyde Martin, converted from a left-handed player to a right-handed player, an extraordinarily complex transition. The hard work paid off, as Adams shot his way onto several leaderboards in black tournaments throughout the country.

Golf did more than satisfy his competitive drive. It also provided the opportunity to build and sustain friendships. Adams was inherently laconic and guarded. As his wife said, Adams didn't "overflow." He didn't exhibit emotion or share information very freely. But rounds of golf with friends, which were quiet, concentrated, and hours long, gave him the chance to open up, to explore issues in a discrete, thoughtful way. Most of the friendships he had owed something to the game of golf, perhaps none more so than his relationship with Louis. Both men bore tremendous pressure in their respective professions, so the golf course represented a mental reprieve as well as an athletic challenge. Adams and Louis spent hundreds of hours together on courses throughout the United States. For example, so anxious was Louis to hit the links with Adams after being honorably discharged from the U.S. Army that he didn't even bother taking off his military uniform before heading to the Adams home to arrange a golf trip. When he arrived, he changed his clothes and told

William and Victorine that he never wanted to see the uniform again. Victorine wouldn't let him throw it out, however. She felt that others would like to see the uniform of the great Joe Louis, so she took possession and promised that she would donate it to a museum. Unfortunately for potential recipients, Victorine never got around to contributing it. Meanwhile, Louis and Adams headed to California, where they spent most of the following 15 days golfing. During one round on a segregated course just outside of Los Angeles, they ran into Jackie Robinson, who was to take the first step in his historic journey to desegregate Major League Baseball the very next day when he reported to the Brooklyn Dodgers' minor league team in Montreal. Adams and Robinson faced off on the golf course again years later, following Robinson's retirement from baseball.

While Robinson had a sweet swing on the baseball diamond throughout his career, "Little Willie Adams," Roger Pippen wrote in his *News-Post* column, "is a sweet putter."

013 INVESTING IN PEOPLE

By 1946, Adams's reputation as a generous supporter of aspiring black professionals and entrepreneurs had spread so widely that he received a regular deluge of proposals. People pitched every kind of idea to him everywhere he went. Some wanted financial help to earn professional degrees to become doctors, dentists, and lawyers. Others sought capital to turn their business ideas into reality. If Adams thought they had the potential to succeed, he invested, believing strongly that the black community needed to build its middle class and to create businesses that would allow Negroes to spend their money with Negroes. When he backed entrepreneurs he almost always did so without asking for a thorough business plan, believing that people were inherently driven and honest. If they set their minds to something and gave their word, they would work tirelessly to succeed. A person's pledge was all he needed. After all, his word was inviolable. A friend would later joke that if Adams telephoned him in the middle of a torrid Baltimore summer and said it was snowing outside, then he would dig his winter coat out of the closet before checking the window to confirm Adams's improbable report. Adams would pay over and over again throughout his life for believing that others shared his devotion to fulfilling commitments regardless of consequences. "When somebody convinced me they could do something, I'd invest or partner with them," Adams later said. "When I chose unwisely, it created debts that I'll never collect on." But Adams was undeterred by the growing pile of IOUs in his office safe.

Adams's own business partner, Henry Parks, also had a proposal in 1946. He had learned from a former college classmate that the owner of a modest but successful food company in Cleveland was interested in raising capital to expand. Adams needed nothing more than Henry's interest to proceed. In the months since they met, Henry more than validated Adams's impetuous open offer of an unspecified professional opportunity. More than a half century later, Adams reflected on what Parks had meant to him. Parks was critical to Adams's drive to exit the number business altogether and devote himself to legal business. Henry had formal business training, which set him far apart from so many at the time. Most of the people who were expressing interest in business were hustlers and gamblers, Adams later recalled, which didn't prepare them very well to succeed. A hustler and gambler himself, Adams wasn't a hypocrite. He believed that he, too, lacked what it took to make it in big-time business. He needed partners like Parks. "I had what Henry didn't, and Henry had what I didn't," Adams observed. "I had the cash, and he had the knowledge."

So Parks and Adams traveled to Cleveland to meet Leroy Crayton, the owner of Crayton Southern Sausage Company Inc. Adams liked what he heard. The company produced a good product, generated an annual profit of $15,000 — more than $1 million in 2015 dollars — and had a lot of room to grow. Adams bought 49 percent of the company from Crayton for roughly $75,000 in cash and put his ownership stake in Parks's name. Crayton and Parks used the cash infusion to open a manufacturing plant in Baltimore, enabling the company to deliver fresh products up and down the East Coast. In addition to the cash investment, Adams donated two adjoining rowhouses that he owned for conversion into a plant. Adams also gave Parks carte blanche. He trusted him to do what was right. He would play no role in the company unless Henry requested his involvement.

While several of his other ventures faltered, Crayton flourished. Within three years, Parks had not only made a success of the Baltimore location. He also had opened new facilities in Philadelphia and Washington. Thanks to Parks's deft expansion drive, profits increased exponentially, soaring 566 percent. But problems emerged. Adams, for one, was growing frustrated by Crayton's unwillingness to share any of the company's profits in the form of dividend payments. As a result, Adams's money generated no return. It was turning out to be a bad deal after all, but one he was willing to tolerate as long as Parks remained committed. But eventually, Crayton also alienated Parks, the man who was making him rich. Like so many companies at the time, Crayton relied on the hands of his employees, rather than machines, to produce his product. Following a standard inspection, the Baltimore City Health Department informed Parks that he had to overhaul his Baltimore operation. The current hands-on method violated sanitation standards. In response, Parks devised a modernization plan that would bring the company into compliance and increase efficiency. Crayton refused, unwilling to invest profits. And since he owned 51 percent of the company, Crayton's word was decisive. The decision made no sense to Parks or Adams. The Health Department had the power to shut them down. This wasn't really their decision to make. They had to change their ways. The only question was how.

Seemingly trapped between Crayton and the government, Parks decided the time had come to part ways. Confident that he could build an even more successful company on his own, Parks left Crayton. Equally confident in Parks's ability, Adams followed suit, asking Crayton either to buy out his position or to permit him to sell it on the open market. Crayton agreed to return half of Adams's initial investment, but he refused to refund any more. It is impossible to determine Crayton's motivation. Perhaps he reasoned that Parks would be unable to create a viable competitor without major backing from Adams, backing that would be harder for Adams to provide without all of the money he invested in Crayton. If this was Crayton's calculation, he was wrong. Adams could afford to invest in his protégé without first collecting the roughly $38,000 owed to him by Crayton.

Leroy Crayton may have withheld the money for another reason. Having worked with Adams for a number of years, Crayton must have been aware of Adams's exaggerated sense of frugality. The same man who shared his wealth so generously to help others was, in his personal dealings, almost farcically economical. All of his associates experienced it at one time or another. "I've seen him drop a penny on the floor and look all over God's creation for it," Henry Parks said. "On trips, I'll suggest a parlor car, and he'll say, 'Let's ride in the coach.'" Some years later, he would persistently circle the block in his car looking for a parking meter with time remaining rather than pull into a more convenient garage and pay himself.

Like so many people shaped by the Great Depression, Adams was invariably and almost excessively thrifty. Crayton would have known this. While Adams could have afforded to walk away from the money owed to him, he was, perhaps, psychologically incapable of doing so. What's more, it was not Adams's style to be adversarial, regardless of his feelings. Therefore, he likely wouldn't make an appreciable investment in a Crayton competitor while trying to recoup money from Crayton. That would be very bad business diplomacy. Indeed, during this period, Adams maintained a relatively warm personal relationship with Crayton, inviting him and his wife to spend time with the Adamses at their beach home on the Chesapeake Bay.

014 DAWN OF THE ENDLESS PURSUIT

Crayton wasn't Adams's only interest as the 1940s drew to a close. By 1949, William and Victorine had lived two stories above Little Willie's Inn for more than a decade. While Adams had invested to make his home and tavern jewels in Baltimore's inner city, he wanted more. He had worked hard and earned enough to buy a single-family home in the neighborhood of his choosing. But in this, the law — not money — represented the barrier to entry. Like cities and states across the nation, Baltimore City maintained so-called restrictive covenants legally prohibiting Negroes from living outside of designated areas, all of them located in densely populated and inferior neighborhoods. In 1948, Baltimore's Thurgood Marshall and others challenged the constitutionality of restrictive covenants in court, picking up an unexpected supporter in the campaign. More than 20 years earlier, while serving as Baltimore's city solicitor, Philip Perlman fought to preserve the city's housing policy of segregation. But in 1948, as the U.S. solicitor general,

Perlman reversed directions, arguing before the Supreme Court of the United States, in the combined cases of *Shelly v. Kraemer* and *McGee v. Sipes*, that racially restrictive covenants breached the Constitution and should be demolished. The nation's top court agreed, opening the door for Negroes to move where they wished. What the Supreme Court could not do was ensure the safety of colored people with the courage to move into all-white neighborhoods.

Despite the danger involved, Adams wasted no time. A friend was in the process of constructing a couple of houses in one of the city's wealthiest all-white neighborhoods, Lake Ashburton. Residents included Jerold Charles "Jerry" Hoffberger, the president of the National Brewing Co. who would later become part owner of the Baltimore Orioles. The builder sold one house with the intention of moving into the second home himself. But when he ran out of cash, he put the house up for sale. The best offer he received was $22,000. To compensate the white builder for the controversy sure to ensue for having sold to a black man, Adams paid a premium of more than 20 percent for a total of $27,000 for the house in the 3300 block of Carlisle Avenue.

Adams initially planned to retain ownership of the building that housed Little Willie's Inn, but he could not find someone to run the tavern. The business had gotten to be too much for his father-in-law, Joseph, so he sold the Whitelock building in all-black Sugar Hill. Shortly thereafter, he financed a new bar for his father-in-law, Little Joe's.

If Adams feared that his pioneering move into an all-white neighborhood would put his family's safety in jeopardy, he didn't disclose it. But many years later, he revealed his belief that the move to Lake Ashburton had cost him dearly. Some in Baltimore's powerful white establishment, he maintained, were so offended by what they perceived as his imperious intrusion that they made it their life's work to bring Adams down. And the conspirators launched their effort immediately, he asserted.

On Saturday, November 19, Adams arrived late for an early afternoon meeting in West Baltimore. In fact, he often ran behind schedule. Some of his closest friends and associates joked that Adams's only flaw was a chronic inability to be on time. They happily overlooked the shortcoming because Adams was otherwise unfailingly reliable. At 3:45 p.m., he rang the doorbell at 2006 West North Avenue, a two-story rowhouse, and waited for someone to admit him. That someone was entirely unexpected and yet immediately identifiable.

"Police!" shouted Patrolman Hubert Hogan, standing just inside the opened door. Rather than enter, Adams bounded down the front steps and started walking away. He didn't get far. Hogan quickly reached and arrested him. Police raided the house more than an hour earlier, at 2:30 p.m., having received a tip that a group of numbers figures would be meeting there. The information proved correct. In the narrow home, police discovered 17 people, multiple adding machines, a couple of cigar boxes full of money, and several locked boxes made of steel. To open the padlocks, police methodically tried every key possessed by every suspect on the premises, one after another. None of them worked. None, that is, until they tried Adams's keys. All told, authorities seized numbers slips for nearly 270,000 bets, accounting for precisely $43,284.56 in money wagered, and arrested everyone on site, including Adams and his father-in-law, Joseph Quille. In addition to the keys, Adams was carrying $2,000 in denominations of $50 and $100, as if he had just withdrawn the cash from the bank.

Police and prosecutors concluded that they had confiscated six days' worth of betting, Monday through that Saturday, and therefore charged Adams with six counts of violating the state gambling law. Adams pleaded not guilty, despite the fact that only his keys opened the strongboxes. His odds of victory, already seemingly long, appeared to worsen when the presiding judge enthused about the potential of the case before him. "This may be an opportunity to break up the headquarters of an organization that may be spread out all over Baltimore City," Judge Michael J. Manley said. Manley was correct, but Adams's lawyers, Joseph H. A. Rogan and J. Francis Ford, had no intention of basing their case on the question of innocence or guilt. Instead, they challenged the legal validity of the police search and arrest. Judge Manley ultimately conceded their argument, ruling that the search-and-seizure warrant was unconstitutionally vague and that Adams hadn't been seen doing anything illegal. The fact that Adams visited a home clearly serving as a numbers headquarters did not justify his arrest, Manley concluded. With their case against Adams seemingly lost, the authorities took a new approach. Patrolman Hogan said he didn't arrest Adams under the warrant. Instead, he arrested him for assault. Hogan said that Adams pushed him after he identified himself as a police officer. A fellow officer who participated in the raid,

Willie Runyon, confirmed Hogan's account. Adams disputed Hogan's story, saying that it was Hogan who physically tried to pull him into the house. If Hogan had lured or forced Adams inside, then the warrant would have applied to him. But it was not to be. Adams slipped through the state's hands, winning an acquittal in March 1950. The same was not true for most of the others who attended the meeting. Sixteen people were convicted and received the most severe punishment in the history of Baltimore's numbers cases, according to *The Sun* newspaper. Judge Manley handed out jail time totaling nearly 1,000 days and fines totaling $14,090. Nobody paid a steeper price than Walter Rouse, who pleaded guilty to all six counts to take responsibility for the entire operation, according to his lawyer. The court sentenced him to 90 days in prison and levied a $2,450 fine. Rouse's lawyer described his client as a legitimate businessman "who got the foolish notion that there was more money in the numbers business."

Despite the severe punishment meted out by Judge Manley, prosecutors in the case were not satisfied. The biggest fish was Adams, not Rouse, and they weren't going to let him get away without exhausting every option. Further analysis of evidence confiscated at the alleged racket headquarters by the officer in charge of the raid, Captain Alexander Emerson, produced a stunning discovery. More than 90 numbers writers forwarded their collections to the raided building. This was a major operation, totaling roughly 1,000 workers in all. So the state filed an appeal, challenging the lower court's decision to dismiss the charges against Adams. Adams's lawyers balked, deriding the attempt as a blatant violation of their client's constitutional double jeopardy rights. In November 1950, Maryland's highest court agreed with Adams. Judge Charles Markell ruled that there are exceptions to the state's ban on double jeopardy cases, but Adams's wasn't one of them.

Only a bravura performance by his lead lawyers, Ford and Rogan, kept Adams out of jail and in business. Whether they knew it or not, the police had in fact infiltrated Adams's sprawling numbers operation when they raided 2006 North Avenue. This in itself was no small accomplishment. Adams regularly relocated his headquarters from house to house in hopes of keeping authorities off of his tail. He didn't use occupied homes for fear that the owner and renter would be prosecuted. Aware that he was under police surveillance, he carefully handled everything related to the numbers. He wouldn't allow so much as a numbers slip into his home or one of his businesses. The likelihood of a raid was too high, and he didn't want to give anybody reason to suspect that his legal businesses were fronts for his gambling operation. Numbers operators commonly opened bars and nightclubs to effectively serve as retail locations for the numbers.

Adams took other precautions, as well. He expanded his numbers enterprise by creating partnerships rather than by hiring an ever-larger roster of employees. He wanted to give participants a greater stake in the business to prevent them from stealing or being indiscreet. Partners had more reason to protect money and information. Employees who felt unappreciated or underpaid were too likely to steal or leak.

And, of course, Adams had a way with the police, a way paved with money and favors. Perhaps not so coincidentally, Adams and one of the officers who participated in the raid maintained a close relationship for the next half century. Adams even attended the wedding of the man's daughter. But despite all these measures, only exceptional legal representation by Ford and Rogan — Governor Herbert O'Conor's former law partner — enabled him to remain a free man. It wouldn't be the last time they would narrowly preserve his freedom.

015 BIRTH OF A BREAKTHROUGH

By 1951, Henry Parks could no longer resist his unmistakable calling. Since leaving Crayton Sausage, he had worked for Adams on a variety of initiatives. While appreciative for the work, Parks, now 34 years old, wanted — needed — to open and operate a company of his own. A true entrepreneur unsuited to serving as a subordinate, Parks knew exactly how he was going to fulfill his need: by going head-to-head with his former business partner, Leroy Crayton. Parks launched a food products company, H.G. Parks Inc. Crayton, Parks believed, was too stupid, too greedy, or both to seize the lucrative business opportunity right in front of him. Parks had tried to help him, but Crayton refused. Now Parks intended to make him pay.

To get his new company off of the ground, Parks gambled the roof over his head and the insurance on his life, having nowhere else to turn for sufficient capital, he maintained. It is true that Parks could not turn to a bank for financing. That route was foreclosed to him because of his race. No lending institution in Baltimore or elsewhere would issue a business loan to a black man, regardless of the potential profitability of his plan. However, Parks did not go it alone by cobbling together only $60,000 by taking out a second mortgage and draining his insurance policy, as he publicly proclaimed. In fact, Adams, 37, covertly staked Parks by devising a cunning financial strategy that would be widely employed and modified on Wall Street in subsequent decades.

For a number of possible reasons, Adams resolved to provide Parks with the money he needed without leaving any detectable fingerprints on the deal. Although he was still working toward his high school diploma at a nearby night program, Adams developed a solution worthy of a whole faculty of business school professors. Bankers were unwilling to extend credit to black customers. But would they be willing to buy a new collateralized financial instrument if the underlying asset came in their favorite shade of green, rendering the interest-generating investment risk-less? Adams didn't shop the idea around. Instead, he took it to a Baltimore bank executive with whom he had forged a strong relationship, John A. Luetkemeyer Sr. at the Equitable Trust Co. The two first got to know each other in 1938. At the time, Adams banked at the Equitable branch where Luetkemeyer worked as manager. Now, 13 years later, Adams pitched his novel deal to Luetkemeyer, now the institution's president. Adams would fill a safe deposit box with his cash and turn the key over to the bank, thereby creating a line of credit with no downside for the lender. The bank's profit was assured. It could collect from Parks or from the box stored in its safe. Adams's banker accepted.

It wouldn't be the last time. "He has signed notes for others, and I was very impressed that on several occasions when the people were not successful, he paid the note off as agreed, like a clock," Luetkemeyer said years later. "He never winced." In subsequent decades, Adams used the same collateralized instrument to finance all kinds of endeavors, including political campaigns.

Adams never revealed the reasoning behind his decision to keep his involvement confidential. But plausible explanations abound. One, of course, is that discretion was Adams's preferred mode of operation. Throughout his life, he maintained a low profile, and he insisted on the same from his associates. One observer quipped that Adams's people could be identified by the inconspicuous cars they drove, Buicks rather than Cadillacs. Another possible motive rests in Henry Parks's astute analysis of consumer behavior. Parks understood something ugly, yet fundamental, about the marketplace in the years following World War II. The challenges facing a black company in a market dominated by whites and segregation were formidable enough. No margin for error existed. Without a sterling reputation, a black-owned company was all but lost, Parks recognized. In later years, he would berate staff if he saw even a small patch of brown grass in the lawn fronting his headquarters building. He also had his delivery trucks washed every day, believing that he needed to cultivate a spotless public image for his company. It would be consistent, then, that he wanted to create distance between his company and the prime purveyor of illegal gambling. Backing from Adams — famous to some, infamous to others — could besmirch his company.

Regardless, Adams continued to back him privately. With financing in place, they turned their attention turned to locating and securing real estate appropriate for manufacturing. For this, Adams tapped another business connection. A liquor distributor with whom Adams had done business for many years owned a building on Pennsylvania Avenue 10 blocks north of The Club Casino. He operated his business out of half of the facility, while the remaining half stood empty, having been vacated by a small dairy company. As a favor to Adams, an important client, the owner offered Parks terms that he couldn't refuse, because there were no terms. Write your own lease and set the rate of rent that you are willing and able to pay, he said, and I'll sign it.

Next, Parks went to work recruiting talent. He could and would consult Adams on overarching strategic matters, but he needed managers to help with day-to-day operations. This seemingly simple task was complicated by the matter of race. Parks needed experienced professionals. But whites with experience were unwilling to work for a black owner, and precious few Negroes, who were willing and eager to work for Parks, possessed any background in management. Where, after all, could a Negro earn such experience? The overwhelming majority of companies were owned and operated by whites. And they weren't about to dilute their power by sharing it with Negroes. Even whites with a social conscience had reason to preserve the racial hierarchy, for if they challenged the status quo and promoted a Negro to a position of real responsibility, then they too might face the wrath of those opposed to integration. Parks eventually found an exception in Raymond V. Haysbert, who was teaching business courses and running the bookstore at Wilberforce University, the oldest private Negro college in the nation. Parks asked Haysbert whether he would be interested in coming to Baltimore from Ohio to discuss the possibility of joining his company. Some 50 years later, Haysbert could still vividly recall his first meeting with Adams and Parks, mostly because of where they met.

In addition to a preternatural ability to crunch numbers, Adams had an uncommon vision for real estate development. Through multiple acquisitions of shack-strewn, overgrown parcels of land along the shores of the Chesapeake Bay, he pieced together a swath of property sizable enough to accommodate his plan for a warm-weather counterpart to the Pennsylvania Avenue entertainment corridor. After clearing away the detritus, he constructed a sprawling pavilion and a stage to host musical performances. Elsewhere on the property, he erected amusement rides and installed slot machines. In no time, Carr's Beach was a sensation, becoming one of the most popular destinations on the East Coast for Negroes. The disc jockey Hoppy Adams selected Carr's Beach as the home for his national radio show, "Bandstand on The Beach." Among those who graced Adams's stage during the live show every Sunday at 3 p.m. were Ella Fitzgerald, Etta James, Lloyd Price, Little Richard, James Brown, The Shirelles, and The Drifters.

"I was amazed," Haysbert said of his interview at Carr's Beach, "because I had never seen that many black people congregated in an entertainment venue before. I was even more amazed when I saw people carrying bags of money while surrounded by guards." After assessing the scene at Carr's Beach, Haysbert concluded that the opportunity to join Parks and Adams was too big to pass up. These were major players, he believed, and so he signed on as plant manager and moved to Baltimore.

But the plant was the least of their worries. Parks had mastered the production process during his time at Clayton. The real challenge now was convincing grocers to stock and sell his product. The problem wasn't quality. Parks tasted the sausage daily, and he became legendary for his ability to detect even a few too many ounces of salt in a 400-pound batch. He was so good, in fact, that the staff would on occasion secretly test him, throwing in a dash too little of this or that. Without fail, Parks identified the mistake. And his quality controls were unprecedented in business. They had to be. One bad batch, and Parks Inc. was over.

The present issue was race, as usual. Parks had little trouble persuading black store owners to carry his sausage, but they captured an inconsequential fraction of the overall market, in part because they were few in number. There just weren't many black-owned stores. But this was only part of it. Black consumers, by and large, preferred to shop at white-owned stores, believing that white stores generally offered higher quality products than black-owned competitors. As a result, Parks needed to get his sausage into white-owned stores, and that would take something akin to a miracle. White grocers didn't have much incentive to do business with Parks. They already had perfectly edible and salable sausage in their refrigerators, all provided by vendors whose skin color wouldn't offend customers.

A master marketer, Parks went to work on a plan to hurdle the obstacles he faced. He settled on a two-part initiative. First, he needed to get in the door and meet with grocers. If he gained entry, then he needed to offer a deal that they could refuse only at their own expense. To execute part one, Parks hit the streets. With a comprehensive knowledge of the black consumers from his days working for Pabst, Parks showed up wherever he could find fellow Negroes willing to sample his sausage. He would serve them in church parking lots and parks. Wherever. If he could foster sufficient demand for his food, he might force white grocers to pay attention. If black shoppers started asking for Parks's sausage in large enough numbers, then white owners might at least give Henry Parks a hearing. And his closing argument was convincing, so convincing in fact that some store owners may have questioned Parks's business acumen, if not his sanity. Parks eliminated nearly all of the risk for the grocers. Merchants needed only to pay for the product. After that, they were finished. They didn't have to so much as touch it. All they had to do was make room for it. If it didn't sell, Parks would send his own men to pick it up and replace it with fresh meat. Parks recognized the excess of his offer, but he determined that he had no choice if he wanted to be anything more than a small-time operator. He took the gamble out of necessity.

As Parks worked with grocers, Adams worked the back channels, making off-the-books purchases for the company, such as billboard advertisements. Adams's behind-the-scenes, unaccounted investments helped Parks begin to construct what is known as a fortress balance sheet. That is, the company took on no debt, making it less vulnerable to the vagaries of the economy and consumer tastes.

During it all, Adams made time for his studies, and on June 13, 1951, he collected his high school diploma during the 24th annual commencement for the Frederick Douglass Evening High School. Adams had completed the "academic track" as opposed the "commercial," "dressmaking," or "home nursing" tracks, and he had done so with distinction. Of the 54 academic-track graduates, 11 earned honors, including Adams. During the years following graduation, Adams took classes at four colleges: Cortez Peters School of Business, McCoy College, Morgan State University, and Johns Hopkins University. But despite his admiration for, and devotion to, formal education, he didn't complete his college studies. He also never treated his college classmates as anything less than peers. One fellow student who went on to work for Adams recalled Adams as invariably modest, even in the classroom. "You'd never know he had a dime to his name because of his humble demeanor," said Evelyn Beasley. What's more, she said, "Our teachers may have known the books, but he knew the real world." And he also believed in sharing what he had, she said. Adams offered all of the graduates at Cortez Peters the opportunity to buy clothing at his Pennsylvania Avenue retailer, Charm Center, at greatly reduced prices. "I got a beautiful dress. I couldn't have afforded it without his 'sale.' The same was true for my classmates." Beasley went on to become a teacher and a principal, where she taught the daughter of Henry Parks, among others

When asked why he invested the time and energy to earn an education after he was already firmly ensconced as a successful and powerful businessman, Adams turned dismissive, as if the answer were obvious. "I wasn't so busy that I couldn't find time to go to school," he said. "I wanted to understand things better, and I needed to go to school."

But Adams was about to get much busier.

016 CONGRESS CALLS

Just four weeks after Adams earned his high school diploma, the Congress of the United States summoned him to Washington, D.C. In the U.S. Capitol building at 10:15 a.m. on Monday, July 2, 1951, U.S. Senator Lester C. Hunt called the highly anticipated hearing to order and asked the day's star witness to stand and be sworn in.

"Do you solemnly swear," Hunt intoned, "the testimony you will give this committee will be the truth, the whole truth, and nothing but the truth, so help you God?"

"I do," William Adams pledged.

The lawmakers and aides in attendance had good reason to be skeptical. As members of a rare Senate special committee, which are created only in times of great national crisis, they had by this day spent more than a year investigating organized crime in America. They had spent hours on end listening to suspected underworld figures regale them with an incessant array of conspicuous lies and tortured evasions, all delivered after taking the very same oath of honesty and candor. But Congress and the country were undeterred. Evidence strongly suggested that organized crime was metastasizing, putting the future of America in jeopardy. Cities, in particular, appeared to be at real risk. Ruthless gangster syndicates, with the purchased cooperation of corrupt politicians, police, and other authorities, were taking over and ravaging urban life, using illegal gambling proceeds to finance other nefarious operations. And one of their newest endeavors made their previous efforts in running numbers and bootlegging alcohol look innocuous in comparison. Now they were building networks to import and distribute drugs. The potential for profit was unprecedented. Likewise the potential for human devastation.

Desperate for help to combat such a formidable and malicious foe, many big-city mayors pleaded for help from President Harry S. Truman. He responded by deploying his Justice and Treasury departments. Justice launched racket squads, while Treasury started looking into the income tax returns of suspected gangsters. But by the time Truman, in February 1950, attributed the crime wave to widespread juvenile delinquency caused by families broken up by World War II, the public and press had lost patience and called on Congress to intervene. For the legislator with higher aspirations and no reliance on inner-city political machines with underworld ties, the fight to combat crime packed the potential to change a career. A little-known senator from Wisconsin was, at that very time, deciding which issue to try to ride to re-election: crime or Communism. But Joseph R. McCarthy was outmaneuvered on the crime issue by a faster-moving colleague and so infamously launched a witch hunt for alleged Communists in U.S. government. Meanwhile, the "victor," Estes C. Kefauver, sought to position himself as the country's No. 1 anti-crime crusader. Having defeated Tennessee's state machine to win his first race for Senate in 1948, the Democrat already had designs on the White House just two years later. The special committee he worked to create in 1950 to investigate the underworld and corrupt public officials served him famously. The publicity generated by the hearings vaulted him into contention for the Democratic nomination in 1952. He even outpolled President Truman, an undeclared candidate, in the New Hampshire primary before ultimately going down to defeat to Adlai Stevenson.

By the summer of 1951, the fortunes of Kefauver and the special committee appeared to be heading in opposite directions. On two separate occasions, Congress extended the committee's deadline for a final report to allow for a deeper, wider probe. Kefauver viewed the decision as a mistake. They had investigated enough. The public was focused and hungry for a remedy. To continue with hearings would risk losing momentum for legislation, he argued. When he was effectively overruled, he asked to be excused from the committee. Denied this, too, he compromised, stepping down as chairman but staying on as a member. On July 2, as Senator Hunt began the hearing, neither Kefauver nor the new chairman was even in the room. But outside the room, interest remained high. Barred from admission, reporters huddled in the hallway, hoping to learn anything about the proceedings taking place behind closed doors. They were to miss quite a show.

Before opening the floor for questions, Senator Hunt

asked Adams's lawyers to identify themselves. Joseph H.R. Rogan said that he and his associate, J. Francis Ford, were members of the Baltimore bar and had represented the witness for the last 10 to 12 years. Indeed, Rogan and Ford were responsible for helping Adams to elude conviction following the 1949 raid on his numbers headquarters. Rogan assured the Senate committee that their presence shouldn't be perceived as a signal that their client intended to hide behind the law.

"He desires to fully cooperate," Rogan said. We're only here, he explained, because our client is under a separate federal investigation into his income tax returns. Our hope today is to keep him from saying something that might incriminate him in the other investigation, not this one.

"Thank you very kindly," Hunt responded. "You will be at liberty to advise your client any time you wish."

Hunt turned the hearing over to the committee's associate council, Downey Rice, a former FBI agent, to conduct the questioning. "Will you state your name?" Rice asked.

"William Adams," he said.

Although correct, the response clearly displeased Rice.

"Have you been known by any other names?"

"They call me Willie."

Again dissatisfied, Rice pressed: "Do they call you Little Willie?"

"That is right," Adams conceded, before explaining why he had failed to bring tax records with him as Congress had demanded.

Rice's frustration turned to exasperation, as Adams

delivered a convoluted explanation about an Internal Revenue Service investigation that effectively preempted him from complying with Congress. Adams got a temporary reprieve when Rice stopped the interrogation to announce the late arrival of Senator Herbert R. O'Conor, the committee's new chairman. The organizational realignment appeared more than fortuitous for Adams. O'Conor wasn't just from Maryland, Adams's adopted home state. He was also the former law partner of Adams's attorney, Joseph Rogan. And in December 1946, he had appointed Victorine Q. Adams to the board of the Training School for Colored Girls of Glen Burnie. O'Conor, himself, had been appointed chairman by Democrats concerned that the committee would expose Democratic ties to underworld figures such as Adams. Because O'Conor hailed from a state widely known to have a thriving criminal racket, they expected him to go easy. But Democrats could not go so far as to have O'Conor preside over hearings dealing with Marylanders, so O'Conor recused himself. But he sat in and participated, nevertheless.

With O'Conor recognized, Rice immediately renewed his demand to know why Adams felt free to ignore the order of Congress. Adams's lawyer, Rogan, jumped to his defense, but Senator Hunt cut him off before he could complete a sixth word. You may advise your client, but you may not speak for him, Hunt sniped. Well prepared by his counsel, Adams said he didn't bring his 1950 tax return for fear that it would incriminate him in the IRS investigation. Round and round Rice and Adams went about why Adams didn't provide records for years not under investigation. Having had enough, Rice requested support from the top-ranking elected official: "I am going to ask the Chair to direct the witness to produce copies of his Federal tax returns for the year 1950. Will you comply with that directive? Rice asked.

"No, sir."

"On what grounds?"

"For fear that they might incriminate me."

Rice persisted, asking Adams why he didn't at least bring returns from the early 1940s. Same reason, Adams said.

"Have you ever heard of the statute of limitations?"

"I have heard of it, but I do not understand it."

"You do not understand it. Perhaps counsel could help you with the state of limitations," Rice said. "Would you be good enough, Mr. Rogan, to advise him on that?"

Rogan proved no more helpful, and his responses cast some light on why he and his client were concerned.

"Mr. Rice, is there any limitation insofar as criminal prosecution is concerned?"

Six years, Rice answered.

"How about fraud," Rogan asked.

Six years.

"I do not know whether I can agree with you on that, Mr. Rice."

Wanting to bring an end to the wrangling over records, Senator Hunt compromised: Deliver a copy of your 1942 tax returns, which aren't under IRS investigation, within one week, and we'll move on. Adams relented.

Rice next attempted to make sense of Adams's labyrinth of business concerns. Nightclubs. A seashore amusement park. Real estate in Baltimore, Chicago, and

Winston-Salem, North Carolina. Ladies clothing. Jukebox vendor. Soft drink bottler. Sausage manufacturer. At every stop, Rice pressed Adams for financial specifics. Adams repeatedly begged off, explaining that he didn't keep track of the financials. Incredulous, Rice demanded to know how Adams tracked the money he either made or lost. Adams said he relied entirely on trusted partners who ran all but his real estate office. And then, without transition, Rice cut to the heart of matters, asking Adams whether he knew Sergeant Hiram Butler of the ... Yes, he knew him. In fact, all of black Baltimore recognized Butler's name, at the very least. He broke the color barrier 13 years earlier by becoming the department's first uniformed black officer. But Adams knew Butler better than most, and Rice knew it. After establishing that Adams was close to Butler, Rice asked if they'd taken any trips together. Yes, they'd gone rabbit hunting. Did you ever give him a bottle of liquor? Adams said he didn't know if he had personally, but perhaps he'd received some "from the place." Butler's beat regularly took him past several of Adams' businesses on Pennsylvania Avenue, including the Club Casino. "From the Club?" Rice pursued.

"I wouldn't say offhand."

"As a gift, you mean?"

"I say I wouldn't know if it was. It would be more or less, I guess."

"As a matter of fact, you know about it, don't you? You know about him getting some liquor from there?"

"I wouldn't say one way or the other."

If Rice thought he could establish this small bribe and move on to bigger things, he was mistaken.

Adams denied giving Butler money or Christmas gifts. He also denied helping him with a real estate transaction. Rice's investigatory homework produced nothing of real value, so he turned to Adams's brush with death and the mob. Although 13 years had passed since the bombing, and despite the fact that everybody knew by now that the mob's objective was to take a percentage of his numbers business, Adams remained evasive in response to questioning. When asked if he could identify one of the alleged perpetrators, Julius "Blinky" Fink, for instance, Adams said only: "I think so." This despite the fact that he had stood shoulder to shoulder with him in repeated court hearings and identified him as one of the two men who threatened him. What's more, the two men almost certainly saw each other in the halls of Congress that day. Fink was to be the very next person to testify. Thwarted again, Rice abandoned specific questions and turned to general matters, asking Adams to explain the difference between the "night number" and the "big number." Adams answered that he was unfamiliar with both terms. If Rice had hoped Adams would give him a verbal tour of the numbers business, then it appeared that those hopes were about to be dashed. But Rice persisted, and that persistence yielded a shocking revelation and a piece of information that would be used to stalk Adams all of the way to the Supreme Court of the United States.

"How does the number come up?" Rice continued. "Where do they get it from? Let's say 372 was the number yesterday."

Again, Adams pleaded ignorance: "I don't know."

"Suppose 372 was the number yesterday, how would they get it?"

"When I was in," Adams said, "you took it from the races."

Rice either didn't believe what he had just heard or he didn't instantly recognize the significance of the statement, for he didn't immediately pursue it. "From the total mutual at the track?"

"Yes, sir," Adams replied.

"Get it out of the paper?"

"Yes, sir."

"Have they stopped doing that?

"Wouldn't know," Adams answered, again hinting at the inconceivable.

"You say you were in it, when was that?"

Considering how well prepared and how disciplined he had been in his testimony until this point, what Adams delivered next was certainly the product of copious strategizing. If not, one of his lawyers would have interrupted. But neither did.

Adams didn't answer Rice's question directly. He didn't indicate when he was in the numbers. Instead, he said he was no longer involved. "I have been out of it now for some time." Asked to be more specific, Adams said he exited the numbers business the previous year, in May. The assertion made little impression on the Senate committee, whose members had heard hundreds of witnesses make similar proclamations. Asking his first questions of the day, Senator Charles W. Tobey, a New Hampshire Republican, took over for Rice and got right to the point.

"What is your net worth, sir?"

"I wouldn't know, sir," Adams responded.

"Who would know?"

"I don't know of anybody [who] would know?

Toby pressed on: "What is [your] worth represented by — securities, property, and money?"

"I would say I have some stocks," Adams said.

"What are they worth?"

"They are not stocks on the stock market," Adams explained. "It is just private corporations' stock in different things … and a real estate business."

Senator Tobey took a modified approach. "Are you worth half a million dollars?"

"No, sir," Adams said, "way below that."

Assuring Senator Tobey that Adams has been instructed to provide financial records to the committee, Downey Rice resumed questioning. He returned to the numbers, perhaps sensing that Adams was willing to discuss the business now that he had claimed to be out of it. In this, he was correct.

When asked about the whereabouts of his last numbers headquarters, Adams candidly explained that he moved his operation from location to location. He then proceeded to elaborate about the role he played in the business at the end of his tenure. He effectively admitted to being a lay-off man, having turned the day-to-day role of banker over to others. In this capacity, Adams took the big bets that others couldn't cover financially and left the smaller stuff to others.

"What would your total daily book be, the amount of action you were handling a day, when you were in the field going full blast?" Rice asked.

"I guess around close to a thousand dollars a day."

The total dazzled even Rice, who had heard and seen it

all by now. "One thousand dollars a day!" he exclaimed.

"Around that," Adams coolly replied, "a little better sometimes."

"How many people would be betting that in to you, so it would aggregate $1,000 a day?"

Adams said it was all but impossible to determine, and for once he wasn't dissembling. He helpfully explained his answer at length:

"The way I would get it would be as if you were a banker and you were keeping the little stuff and you would give me your package of large stuff, because the writers write more smaller stuff since they get a percentage off that and naturally they get more nickels and pennies and dimes in their plays than they would quarter plays or more, so you would be the one who ordinarily would have control of that," he said of the bets of 25 cents or more. Numbers writers would make arrangements with him via telephone or personal visit, Adams continued.

Adams's performance was surprising and, frankly, more than a little bewildering. The Senate special committee possessed little legal power. Witnesses were required to appear when subpoenaed, or they risked being charged with contempt. Beyond that, they had no obligation to testify. They could simply invoke their constitutional Fifth Amendment protection against self-incrimination. And that is exactly what most witnesses did. So by the summer of 1951, the committee's members had come to expect little in the way of useful information. But here was a witness sharing the inner-most workings of the numbers racket, as well as his revenue. More amazing was the fact that this candid testimony came from a man of very few words, even in the most felicitous of settings. Yet here he was, in front of a hostile investigatory body, expatiating freely about the business. Why? If Rice had questions about Adams's motives, they could wait for later. Finally, he had a seemingly compliant witness, and he wanted to make the most of it.

"Who kept the records for you when you were running that operation?"

"I kept them," Adams said.

"You kept them yourself?"

"Yes, sir."

In this, Rice clearly saw an opportunity to snare Adams, asking one more time: "You did all the bookkeeping?"

And for the first time, Adams swallowed Rice's hook. "I had probably someone who helped me. I wouldn't say I did it all."

"Who would help you?" he followed.

"I had one other person."

"Who was that other person?"

Seeming to stall for the time needed to craft an answer, Adams repeated the question: "Who was the other person?"

"Yes," Rice averred.

"I wouldn't like to do that," Adams said.

"Suppose we direct you to?"

Senator Hunt interjected: "The acting chairman directs you to answer the question."

Demonstrating that he well understood the rules of the game, Adams declined, pleading the Fifth.

Rice made another attempt. Was this person male or

female?

"I have the same answer," Adams said. "I would refuse to answer on the same ground."

Senator Hunt was forced to concede: "There isn't any way we can compel the witness to answer."

With the hearing drawing to a close, Rice returned to Adams's apparent comfort zone. "You say you quit the business about May of 1950. To whom did you turn over your numbers business?

"Not to anyone," Adams said.

"You let it collapse?"

"I wouldn't have anyone working for me. I wouldn't have anybody to turn it over to. I was taking action from the fellows who were giving it to me."

Asked to expand on the answer, Adams again delved into his operations. When betting was particularly heavy on a given number, Adams would insure himself against a major payout by betting on the same three digits with another banker. He would both lose and win, protecting himself from a heavy loss. It was the same kind of hedging tactic that Wall Street investors employed. But once again, Adams refused to name names, saying he couldn't recall who he dealt with in these transactions.

An hour and fifty minutes after swearing Adams in, Senator Hunt excused the witness. Before Adams had a chance to leave the room, Hunt called for the next witness to come forward.

"Would the witness state his name, please."

"Julius Fink."

Fink declined to cooperate, refusing to answer even the most mundane questions. On grounds that it would incriminate him, he declined to tell the committee where he went to grade school, what business he was in, and whether he knew "Willie Adams." Getting nowhere, the committee excused him. For Fink, it was over. For Adams, it was only just beginning.

017 "CONTROLLING LOTTERY FIGURE" INDICTED

The Senate special committee closed the July 2, 1951, session to the public and press, presumably to encourage witnesses to be forthcoming. But when most of the day's witnesses refused to cooperate, the committee's staffers, Downey Rice and Richard G. Moser, turned to the media for help. During a recess, Rice and Moser went out into the hallway where reporters were gathered hoping to pick up any information at all about the day's big story and delivered the theme they wanted splashed on the front pages of the newspapers. The *Evening Sun*, published just hours after the hearings concluded, opened its front-page story with words that captured what Rice and Moser were up to.

"Threats of contempt-of-Congress citations were brandished before four balking kingpins of Baltimore's sporting world today in an attempt to wring from them facts about gambling rackets in the city." To their credit, reporters raised questions about the government's ability to fulfill the threat, citing "legal tangles" related to the constitutional protection from self-incrimination. Rice and Moser told the press that only Adams among the day's witnesses had "talked quite freely about a lot of things." For instance, Moser said, Adams told them that he earned an average of $1,000 a week from the numbers business from 1942 until 1950. But that wasn't exactly what Adams had said. Instead, he reported that he generated $1,000 per day, not per week. And that $1,000 wasn't necessarily earnings, it was revenue. And he hadn't said the $1,000 was an average from 1942 until 1950. That was the total right around the time he claimed to have left the business. It appears that Rice and Moser were responsible for the mistakes, because several newspapers independently published the exact same account. Had the press revisited what the police recovered during the 1949 raid on Adams's alleged headquarters in West Baltimore, they may have challenged the number. Authorities recovered more than $43,000 for six days' worth of wagers, meaning the organization was grossing an average of $7,200 per day. But ultimately it didn't matter. Whether it was weekly or daily, earnings or profit, $1,000 was a sum big enough to capture the imagination of readers. The paper also reported Adams's assertion that he was no longer involved, that he had gotten out of the numbers altogether.

The following day, a competing newspaper, the *Baltimore News-Post*, published more pointed comments from Moser. Fink was "clearly in contempt," Moser said. "We intend to ask Congress to press these contempt cases vigorously when they are brought formally. We have no intention of letting witnesses walk in here and refuse to testify to anything material." Moser explained that the only reason they hadn't already charged Fink and others with contempt was that they wanted to confirm that the witnesses had been properly subpoenaed and served. "When the committee is satisfied of that, then it will take up the contempt cases."

The committee's chairman, however, struck a different tone than his underlings. Senator O'Conor emphasized that the Senate investigation wasn't a prosecution and that witnesses were in no direct legal danger. The committee's objective, he said, was to collect information that will inform remedial legislation. O'Conor certainly realized that Moser's threats would do nothing but prompt future witnesses to be even less compliant, which would be counterproductive. Moser wasn't the only person complicating matters for the Senate committee. Local prosecutors across the country, including Baltimore's, were beginning to come forward, threatening to use the congressional testimony against the witnesses in their respective jurisdictions.

Less than a month after Adams testified, Baltimore City's State's Attorney Anselm Sodaro announced his intentions to continue the Senate's inquiry on the local level. He summoned 27 people, including Adams, to testify before a grand jury, starting on August 1. "My decision to conduct a grand jury investigation into gambling activities is the result of a conference I had last week in Washington with the Senate crime committee," Sodaro explained. "I am conducting this investigation on a local level which is beyond the scope of the crime committee in Washington."

Sodaro called Adams and all 17 co-defendants from the 1949 raid on Adams's suspected numbers headquarters, as well as Baltimore Police Sergeant James Hiram Butler, the officer Adams had been asked about during his congressional testimony.

Despite being summoned, Adams did not appear before the grand jury on August 1. Adams and his wife were out of town on vacation, his lawyer, Joseph Rogan, explained, but they will return in time for Adams to testify the following day. Discussing day one of the grand jury proceedings with the press, Sodaro disclosed his willingness to give witnesses immunity from prosecution in exchange for their candid testimony. Sodaro did not specify who would receive offers of immunity, but this would become apparent soon enough.

The case Sodaro presented to the Baltimore grand jury relied heavily on Adams's testimony before Congress, despite the fact that he had been unable to obtain a complete record of the proceedings from the federal government. Sodaro had gone to Senator O'Conor and his staff and requested all materials pertaining to Adams. But his request went unfulfilled. He couldn't even secure a complete transcript of Adams's testimony. Moving to buttress his case, Sodaro filed what was then considered an unusual subpoena. He wanted to share Adams's income tax records from 1948, 1949, and 1950 with the grand jury. The state of Maryland complied, sending a representative from the Comptroller's Office to present the tax information. Sodaro made his case to the grand jury, arguing that they had sufficient evidence to bring charges against Adams. After all, Adams had unequivocally confessed to participating in the numbers racket. If Adams's detailed explanation of the numbers business wasn't enough to confirm his involvement, then his earnings certainly were. He admitted to earning $1,000 a week. These weren't the earnings of a low-level functionary. Adams was a kingpin. If the grand jury performed its duty, Sodaro could put the head of a nefarious gambling ring behind prison bars, making the city safer for all. If Adams were incarcerated, his racket just might collapse. Cut off from enormous profits, the argument continued, Adams wouldn't be unable to enter new lines of illegal business, such as prostitution and drug dealing, as major numbers figures were doing in cities throughout the United States. Sodaro proved persuasive.

On August 24, 1951, the grand jury indicted Adams, charging him with two counts of conspiring to violate the state lottery laws. In charge one, he was accused of conspiring with "certain persons unknown to the jurors" to break the state's anti-numbers laws. In the second charge, he was alleged to have broken the same law with a co-defendant whose name the grand jury initially withheld. The co-defendant was Walter Rouse, who took the fall for the 1949 raid, saying he was entirely responsible for the numbers paraphernalia and cash found on the premises. Rouse was indicted on the same two charges. If convicted of both counts, Adams and Rouse faced maximum prison sentences of 20 years.

Adams, however, was clearly Sodaro's most prized quarry. Sodaro referred to him as "the controlling lottery figure in the northwestern section of the city." Sodaro, asking for bail to be set at $10,000, vowed that he would move quickly to bring Adams to trial.

The situation for Adams then went from bad to worse. Less than a week later, on the final day of August 1951, the Senate special committee, which was set to expire in a matter of hours, released its much-anticipated report, and the dramatic findings refocused public attention on the criminal underworld and fomented public anxiety. This was particularly true in Baltimore, given the Senate's dismal assessment of the city.

Gambling thrived in Baltimore, the Senate concluded, and "the situation could not have existed without police knowledge and permission." About Adams in particular, the committee minced no words. Without any qualification, the committee declared that Adams clearly is "one of Baltimore's principal numbers syndicate operators." The report went on: "There is substantial evidence that more than a decade ago, after the end of the Prohibition era, national racketeers began to muscle in on Baltimore gambling. A bombing episode in the thirties involving Julius 'Blinky' Fink, associate of Nig Rosens's Philadelphia mob, and numbers operator 'Willie' Adams, marked the beginning of the effort of out-of-state hoodlums to declare themselves 'in' on Baltimore's lucrative numbers business and other gambling. The investigation developed the fact that the head of one of Baltimore's several large numbers syndicates was directly approached by an out-of-town mobster who stated that his outfit was taking over 75 percent of the Baltimore operation. The muscle man pointed out that even after such a cut there would still be more profit because of enlarged operations. Evidently this 'muscle' succeeded, as the local operator withdrew to less dangerous endeavors."

This was the first public reference to who had been behind the 1938 bombing. Nig Rosen, whose real name was Harry Stromberg, held a position in the pantheon of the nation's biggest, most malicious gangsters. When the heads of the most powerful crime syndicates gathered, Rosen took his place at the table along with Al Capone, Bugsy Siegel, Vito Genovese, and Frank Costello. Rosen maintained his prominence in part by relying on the muscle of his most trusted henchmen. They included Max "Chinkie" Rothman, Samuel "Cappie" Hoffman, Joseph "Little Kirssy" Herman, and Max "Willie" Weisberg, the man who participated in the attack on Adams and whose freedom Adams covertly helped to preserve in exchange for the mob's promise not to interfere with him ever again. Baltimore had come close in 1938 to falling into hands of big-city gangsters.

Considering the inflammatory information contained in the Senate committee's report, Maryland elected officials had no choice but to weigh in. The head of the Maryland state legislature's crime committee, Senator Omar D. Crothers, conceded that the findings were "probably true." The numbers and other types of gambling could not have thrived without the police knowledge and cooperation. As a result, Crothers said his committee would launch an inquiry into police corruption.

Baltimore Mayor Thomas D'Alesandro Jr. said only that he had not received a copy of the Senate report, adding that the city's Police Department was under the jurisdiction of Governor Theodore McKeldin. McKeldin said he would make no comment until had read and studied the report.

Adams now personified the crisis in Baltimore, a fact that State's Attorney Sodaro helped along, intentionally or not, by electing to prosecute Adams before all of the other Baltimore gambling figures who had testified before Congress — all of them white. Adams felt that he was being singled out, and he believed he knew why. Two years earlier, he and his wife moved into an all-white neighborhood populated by some of the city's most affluent and influential citizens. He suspected that neighbors unhappy to have Negroes next door and around the corner applied pressure on various public authorities to get the Adamses out. That pressure, he reasoned, prompted Sodaro to put him at the front of the line. Without question, the issue of race was ever-present. In reporting the story, the newspapers never failed to identify Adams and other blacks as Negroes while remaining silent about the race of white suspects. But Adams's theory is impossible to confirm. Sodaro died in 2002, and those who knew Sodaro, both white and black, described him as a man of unfailing integrity and uncommon civility. Even one of Adams's closest associates held the view that Sodaro's ethics were unimpeachable.

An alternative explanation for why Sodaro targeted Adams first may have had do with the nature of Adams's congressional testimony. He had given the prosecutor something substantive to work with, while other Baltimore-based witnesses, such as George Goldberg and Willis M. King, responded to nearly all questions by pleading the Fifth Amendment. While the color of his skin almost certainly didn't help his legal case, the decision by Adams and his lawyers to testify candidly before the Senate committee appeared to have been a misstep with potentially life-changing consequences. Thirty-seven-year-old Adams now faced the prospect of spending 20 years behind bars.

018 SELF-INCRIMINATION

In the days leading up to his November 19, 1951, trial date, Adams experienced yet another public relations nightmare when the commissioner of the Baltimore City Police Department, Beverly Ober, revealed that he was personally conducting a private investigation into allegations that some of his officers had accepted bribes from gambling figures. Even if Ober didn't produce conclusive evidence, his investigation ensured that the Baltimore newspapers would continue writing about the criminal underworld, which in turn would keep the public focused on people such as Adams. The bright, unblinking public spotlight effectively prevented Adams from negotiating any back-room deals, even if he could mount a persuasive argument to make the criminal case go away. There was no downside for Sodaro to pursue Adams to the end of the world, and that's exactly what he was about to do.

When Commissioner Ober disclosed that he was looking into charges of graft in his department, Sodaro immediately stepped forward, promising to share information that he had gleaned from his ongoing grand jury investigation. Ober also received assistance from the U.S. Senate special committee investigation into organized crime. In October, the committee finally made public the transcript of Adams's July testimony. That transcript, of course, included Adams's acknowledgement that he knew police Sergeant James Hiram Butler "very well." Ober was sure to follow up.

While it appeared the public events were all but conspiring against him, Adams did not recoil from the fight. On November 7, less than two weeks before the scheduled start of his trial, Adams's lawyers, Rogan and Ford, appealed a preliminary order by the presiding judge in the case, Joseph Sherbow. The judge had denied their request for more of the evidence the state intended to present at trial. Believing — or at least hoping — that this was an errant ruling, Rogan and Ford asked the state's highest court, the Maryland Court of Appeals, to reverse Sherbow. To protect themselves from accusations that they were merely stalling, Rogan and Ford filed an affidavit, indicating that the appeal was not a delay tactic but rather the result of a sincere legal disagreement. The Court of Appeals consented to hear the appeal on the first day of their next session, December 4, which effectively postponed Adams's trial.

As scheduled, Rogan and Ford appeared before the seven-member Court of Appeals on December 4. All our client wants and deserves, they argued, is for prosecutors to answer two questions. One, do they intend to present evidence seized during the 1949 raid? And two, are they planning to use the testimony Adams gave to the Senate special committee? The judges didn't wait for Rogan and Ford to complete their arguments. They cut the lawyers off and adjourned the hearing. The legal community perceived the brusque move as a signal that the court intended to dismiss the appeal. Apparently anxious to move forward, State's Attorney Sodaro didn't wait for an official ruling. Shortly after the aborted hearing, Sodaro announced that Adams's rescheduled trial would begin on December 20, and this time the date held.

Five days before Christmas, Sodaro dispatched two prosecutors from his office to make the case against Adams. William H. Maynard and William C. Rogers Jr. opened the hearing with an unorthodox move. They called as their witness not an alleged numbers runner but rather a government employee: J. Nelson Rickards Jr., a representative of the Office of the Comptroller, the agency responsible for assessing and collecting state taxes. He took the stand armed with three sets of Adams's tax returns, those for 1948, 1949, and 1950. The records revealed that Adams and his wife, Victorine, reported taxable income of $59,871.81 in 1948, a prodigious sum that firmly secured the couple's position among the city's upper class. Even more interesting, though, was the source of their earnings. Adams reported that he made $45,216 of that total from "speculations," a term that prosecutors said referred to numbers gambling. In 1949, they reported "other income" of $38,000, and in 1950, the Adams's claimed $18,429 from "speculations," meaning he had all but confessed to earning more than $100,000 during a three-year period from an illegal enterprise, according to prosecutors.

The state also presented an estimate of what Adams's numbers operation generated in annual revenue. Based on what the police had seized at the 1949 raid, prosecutors concluded that Adams's gambling racket produced sales of more than $6.6 million per year. The financial analysis apparently went no further, for the most cursory evaluation would have raised questions. Why, for example, had Adams earned less than one half of one percent of total sales? Was he failing to report all that he made from the numbers? If so, why did he run the risk of reporting any gambling earnings at all? The half measure would likely raise red flags without protecting him from the charge of tax evasion, should auditors dig deeper. Was it possible that "speculations" and "other income" referred to investment income? But Adams's lawyers didn't challenge the state's theory. Instead, they asked the judge to exclude all evidence gathered during the 1949 raid. Their client had already been tried and exonerated on that evidence. To admit it at a second criminal trial amounted to a violation of the Fifth Amendment's double jeopardy protection. What's more, they said, Adams went to the raided house in 1949 not to participate in the numbers but to meet a man interested in buying a home from his real estate company. Adams's co-defendant, Walter Rouse, also asked the court to bar the evidence. In his case, he had already been convicted and punished for his involvement. But Judge Sherbow rejected them both.

The state also relied on the testimony of R. Maurice Jones, a man who told the jury that he entered the numbers business at Adams's invitation in 1947. As a top lieutenant, he managed and maintained records for a significantly large branch of Adam's racket. Those records were stored, he said, in a safe at Adams's real estate office over the Club Casino on Pennsylvania Avenue. Jones said he got out of the numbers a year later, in 1948. Adams later urged him to rejoin him in the numbers, Jones said, but he declined.

The third and final element of the state's case centered on Adams's Senate testimony. What more conclusive piece of evidence could the prosecution present than Adams's clear and unequivocal confession?

The jury answered the question less than 24 hours later, finding Adams and Rouse guilty of violating the state's anti-lottery laws. Judge Sherbow chose not to impose sentences immediately, deciding instead to give both defendants the time to file appeals and releasing them on $10,000 bail each. But Sherbow did not withhold his feelings about the case. The city's first big numbers convictions sent an unmistakable signal to the all. Criminals such as Adams who previously had been "able to hide behind the iron curtain finally have been brought to justice," he declared. "This kind of corrupting influence didn't just happen recently. It was here and all of us are paying for its effects." Sherbow added that the public actually deserved some of the blame for being so complacent about illegal gambling. And he concluded his post-trial comments with praise for the "young, energetic State's Attorney's office, full of life, with a desire to really end this kind of situation." Sodaro had not only won. He'd received a very public commendation from one of the city's most reputable authorities. It was looking more likely that Adams's future would include time in jail.

019 THE GAVEL FALLS; THE BETRAYER CALLS

Christmas 1951 could not have been a particularly joyous time at the Adams household. Quickly approaching the end of the legal line, Adams stood convicted of a crime that carried a lengthy prison term. Even worse, the highest court in the state had already considered and dismissed two seemingly strong legal arguments: that he shouldn't be tried a second time on evidence from the 1949 raid and that his Senate testimony should not be admissible. But Adams didn't capitulate. The day after Christmas, Adams and Rouse filed yet another round of appeals.

Adams's attorneys took issue with almost every component of the state's case. To begin with, the prosecution should not have been permitted to introduce Adams's tax returns at trial. That was a clear breach of his constitutional right against self-incrimination. It amounted to Adams testifying against himself, they claimed. Second, prosecutors should not have been allowed to use Adams's

Senate testimony against him. To secure that testimony, Congress granted their client immunity from prosecution. The state of Maryland was effectively and blatantly defying the federal government. And finally, Rogan and Francis took one more legal swing at the evidence collected during the 1949 raid. How could the court possibly conclude that this didn't amount to double jeopardy, they asked?

For more than a month, Adams and Rouse waited for the Supreme Bench of Baltimore to rule on their fate. Then, on Saturday, February 2, 1952, Adams and Rouse received their first piece of good news. A 10-judge panel of the Supreme Bench threw out their convictions, agreeing with their defense lawyers that some of the evidence used against them should not have been permitted. "In our opinion, evidence taken from the income tax returns of the defendant Adams should not have been admitted," the judges wrote. "It is also our opinion that the evidence obtained by the search of the person of Adams was inadmissible because his arrest was illegal. This was also the conclusion of the Court in the trial of Adams in 1950 for violation of the lottery law."

It was now up to the Baltimore's top prosecutor, Anselm Sodaro, to decide whether to retry the cases against Adams and Rouse. Although the Supreme Bench's ruling delivered a blow to the prosecution, could Sodaro accept legal defeat with the entire state watching? The public wouldn't fault him for taking one more shot at a confessed underworld figure. And he still had that confession in his legal arsenal. The Supreme Bench did not respond to the question of Adams's Senate testimony, so he was free to invoke it should he choose to move forward. In previous months, Sodaro had made important decisions and publicly expressed his intentions almost instantly, as he had after the Court of Appeals abruptly halted an earlier Adams appeal. This time, he and his office went silent.

In court almost constantly for the previous 15 months, Adams finally had a little room to breathe. Even if Sodaro decided to try him again, the case against him appeared attenuated, at best. But as he and Rouse waited for Sodaro's next move, the federal government took aim at Adams. A little more than a month after having his conviction thrown out, the United States Internal Revenue Service filed suit against Adams and his wife, seeking back taxes for the years 1947 through 1950. The amount owed: a breathtaking $839,986.95. Even if Adams paid no federal taxes during those years, which is doubtful, then Adams was earning something closer to $250,000 a year, by government estimates, not the $52,000 that he reported to the state of Maryland in 1948. The top federal marginal tax rate fluctuated during those years from 86.45 percent to 84.36 percent. Whatever the true numbers were, there was no doubt that this was a big sum even for Adams. He now had another fight on his hands with the potential to change the course of his life. If he lost, others would certainly suffer.

Not surprisingly, Sodaro decided to continue his pursuit of Adams, announcing on April 8, 1952, that the next trial would begin the following month. This time, a judge, not a jury, would render the verdict. Judge E. Paul Mason may have been more objective or sympathetic than his predecessor, but he was no more receptive to Adams's bid to have his Senate testimony excluded. With less than a week to go before the start of his May 26 trial, Mason said the prosecution would be permitted to introduce the testimony. The judge did, however, grant a request to separate the cases of Adams and Rouse.

Once again, R. Maurice Jones served as a state's witness. This time around, however, he provided more details about his interaction with Adams. As he testified before, he joined the numbers at Adams's behest in 1947. He quit the following year, he added this time, as a result of the increasing difficulty associated with collecting bets. This assertion should have raised a red flag. Few established numbers operators, particularly those backed by Adams, had trouble finding players. Nevertheless, Jones said his mind was made up, so he took what records he had to Adams's office and, not finding him, left them on his desk. For some unexplained reason, Jones decided not to stow them in Adams's safe, just as he said he had done with earlier deliveries during the first trial. Jones proceeded to testify that Adams attempted to re-enlist him on two occasions, first in September 1949 and again in June 1950. This second date, June 1950, could have proved explosive. Adams told Congress that he exited the business in May 1950. Somebody was lying, Adams or Jones. But the obvious discrepancy ultimately proved inconsequential. The prosecutors asked for and received permission to present Adams's Senate testimony and then briskly rested their case. Judge Mason needed nothing further. Adams's second trial ended on day one, as Mason found him guilty of conspiracy to violate the state's lottery laws. Adams's decision to be candid before Congress did him in, Mason conceded. The prosecutors went a step further, identifying the exact piece of testimony that doomed Adams's chance of acquittal. His "one fatal mistake," they said, was his declaration that he quit the numbers in May 1950. Had he identified April 1950 as his final month in business, then the state could not have secured a conspiracy conviction because the two-year statute of limitations would have expired. Adams was convicted on May 26, 1952. The conspiracy charge carried a 10-year prison term. Judge Mason released Adams on $10,000 bail, giving him the opportunity to file another appeal before receiving his ultimate sentence.

Just as he had escaped conviction on a legal technicality two years earlier, he now found himself snared by one, at least in part. And this time, he had but one argument left for an appeal, and it had already been rejected or ignored by every court in the state. If he couldn't convince somebody that his Senate testimony should be inadmissible at trial, then he was headed to jail. It wasn't a matter of if but, rather, how long. Adams filed another appeal with the Supreme Bench, asking them to reconsider. They hadn't addressed the question of his Senate testimony when they ruled to exclude his tax records and evidence from the 1949 raid. Now, it would seem, they had little choice but to address the issue, one way or the other. But once again, the unexpected happened.

The day after the judge ruled against their client, Adams's lawyers, Rogan and Francis, claimed to have received a stunning phone call from Maurice Jones, the man who testified against Adams on two separate occasions. He had a confession to make: He lied on the stand, twice. Adams did not invite him to join his numbers business in 1947. And Jones did not throw numbers records on Adams's desk. Jones added, according to the attorneys, that he wanted to come to their office, recant his earlier testimony, and make his new statement official. Rogan and Ford demurred. Instead, they immediately contacted Judge Mason and city prosecutors to share what had just transpired. Judge Mason instructed the two to redirect Jones to his chambers if he tried to contact them again. He did, and Adams's lawyers passed along the judge's order. But Jones did not appear before Mason.

Rogan and Francis were willing to wait for a matter of weeks but not forever. Jones's admission, if true, might just prompt a judge to declare a mistrial. So on July 11, 1952, the lawyers put their reputations and careers on the line, filing affidavits swearing to the truth of their account of Jones's phone call. Judge Joseph L. Carter responded by issuing an order, giving prosecutors until September 1 to show why the affidavits should not be made part of record in what was sure to be Adams's push for a yet another new trial.

Within a week, Jones publicly dismissed the story of his phone call to Adams's lawyers as a fabrication. Jones said he had not contacted Rogan, Francis, or their secretary at any time. He also stood by the entirety of his testimony against Adams. The prosecutors supplemented Jones's statement with criticism of Adams's lawyers. Rogan and Ford's affidavits were based on "suspicion and conjecture," they said. The claim, though seemingly innocuous and certainly vague, had potentially profound implications. Rogan and Francis's veracity had been called into question. To gain admission to the legal profession, all lawyers must vow to be truthful in all dealings. A failure to fulfill that commitment could lead to a fine, suspension, or even disbarment. If it could be proved that Rogan and Ford prevaricated or even embellished their sworn testimony, then their licenses — and their livelihoods — would be in jeopardy. And even if they were able to remain in good standing with the bar association, their professional reputations would be tarnished, if not ruined. Rogan and Ford knew this. Would they have been willing to risk their careers to falsely besmirch the credibility of a witness? They presumably had a compelling motive. Adams was a significant source of income for both men. They had been working for him nearly non-stop for the last four years. And here they were, in 1952, on the brink of exhausting the last legal means of keeping their client out of jail. So did they lie? Or was it Jones?

Adams first met Reuben Maurice Jones during a visit to Washington, D.C. The young man approached him with a proposal, as so many others did. He wanted to go into business. Would Adams be willing to help? Jones impressed Adams. He seemed smart, driven, and relatively knowledgeable about what it took to run an enterprise. "Back in those days, you didn't find many black people ... who knew anything about business," Adams said years later, recalling his introduction to Jones. Consequently, Adams brought Jones to Baltimore and opened a confectionary store for him to operate in Turner Station, an all-black community bordering the Patapsco River. But Jones foundered at the helm. The failure didn't deter Adams, however. He wanted to give him another opportunity at success, so he established a new tavern where Jones could play a leading role. But again, Jones faltered, prompting Adams to concede the obvious. Jones didn't possess the will or ability to achieve even mediocrity in business. He couldn't continue to throw good money after bad. He had to sever ties with Jones, as painful as it was for him to give up on anyone. Adams had been exceptionally supportive, generous, and patient with Jones. And for that, Jones repaid him with betrayal.

Much of Jones's testimony was fantastically false. Yes, Adams had helped him get into the numbers. But so many of the details he provided were fictitious. For instance, Jones told the court that he often deposited numbers in Adams's safe. Impossible. Nobody but Adams had keys or combinations to his strong boxes and safes. That's where his trust with others ended. And that's why only his keys opened the lock boxes during the 1949 raid.

After the second trial, Jones did, in fact, reach out to Adams and apologize for his false testimony. In addition to forgiveness, he sought reconciliation, entreating his former benefactor to give him one more chance to distinguish himself in a legal business. Adams responded clinically. There was no place for emotion of any kind in business, not even under these extreme circumstances. Jones had three strikes against him — two woefully inept performances in business and his heinous act of disloyalty in court. There would be no fourth. In recalling the incident more than 40 years later, Adams employed the technique that served him well in his criminal enterprise: omission for the sake of discretion and protection. He carefully avoided revealing whom Jones contacted with his apology and plea, Adams or his lawyers. Jones may have felt uncomfortable contacting Adams directly after what he had done and therefore used Adams's lawyers as a back channel. It wouldn't have been wise of him to bring unnecessary participants into the information loop, particularly individuals with an ethical obligation to share it with a judge. But, then, Jones had already conclusively demonstrated with his court testimony that he didn't understand or comply with the criminal code of behavior. One way or the other, Jones admitted that he perjured himself. And in the end, it wouldn't matter who received the confession. On November 26, 1952, the Supreme Bench rejected Adams's appeal and upheld his conviction. Shortly thereafter, on December 2, the court sentenced him to seven years in prison. If he didn't win a long-shot reversal, he would spend the remainder of the 1950s in a penitentiary.

020 ALL THE WAY TO THE SUPREME COURT

With their options dwindling, Rogan and Ford once again asked the Maryland Court of Appeals to overturn Adams's convictions on grounds that his Senate testimony should have been inadmissible. And once again, on June 10, 1953, the state's highest court disagreed, ruling that Adams effectively waived his statutory privilege to immunity by giving his testimony voluntarily. He could have invoked his Fifth Amendment rights and refused to answer the committee's every last question, but he failed to do so. Therefore what he revealed can be used against him in any court of law in the land.

Adams now had only one hope left, and the odds of success were appreciably worse than those for selecting the winning number. He could file an appeal with the nation's highest court, the Supreme Court of the United States. Merely convincing the Supreme Court to accept a case is daunting enough. Every year, the top court receives thousands of hearing requests, known formally as writs of certiorari. From that vast number, the nine justices routinely agree to rule on fewer than 100. To make it onto the docket, a case must present the Supreme Court with the opportunity "to resolve an important question of federal law" or "to review a decision by a lower court that conflicts directly with a previous decision of the Court," among other reasons, according to its rules. Did Adams's appeal meet one of those requirements? Rogan and Ford certainly considered their case worthy of review. After all, if congressional immunity from prosecution applied only to federal prosecution and not state prosecution, then immunity was worthless. But judge after judge in Maryland had ruled otherwise. Rogan and Ford knew they would need help to secure a different outcome at this, their last legal resort. There was nowhere to turn should the Supreme Court rule against them.

With stakes so high, Rogan and Ford encouraged Adams to add George E.C. Hayes to his legal team. As 1952 turned to 1953, Hayes, a graduate of Brown University and the Howard University School of Law, was in high demand. He served as lead counsel in *Bolling v. Sharpe*, a companion case to *Brown v. Board of Education*. He represented Annie Lee Crawford, a federal clerk accused of being a Communist and headed to testify before Senator Joseph McCarthy's committee investigating un-American activities. Hayes responded to Adams's request with an aggressive proposal. For $1,000, he would review Adam's case and decide whether to take him on as a client. If he agreed, an additional financial agreement would need to be negotiated. The sizable sum would guarantee Adams nothing. Hayes could collect, read the record, and then reject Adams as a client without explanation or apology. But with his life on the line, Adams paid, and Hayes ultimately agreed to take the case.

Despite the long odds, the Supreme Court also accepted the case of *Adams v. Maryland*, announcing its decision to do so on October 26, 1953, just three weeks after the former governor of California, Earl Warren, was sworn in as chief justice. The court took on the case because, in the words of Justice Hugo Black, "a proper understanding of the scope of [law pertaining to immunity] is of importance to the national government, to the states and to witnesses summoned before congressional committees."

The pressure was on. The court scheduled oral arguments for January 7, 1954, giving both sides less than 75 days to draft and submit their legal briefs, as well as prepare for the rare opportunity to personally address the nine justices. Except in the most extraordinary cases, Supreme Court hearings are limited to just one hour. As a result, legal briefs are critical. Only in the briefs do lawyers get the chance to state their entire case, to give their interpretation of the relevant statutes and, when necessary, to explore what Congress fully intended when it passed the legislation. Hearings are generally reserved for the judges' questions. This is their opportunity to probe deeper and to challenge the lawyers on both sides.

The Adams legal team was the first to submit a brief, filing the nearly 10,000-word document at the Supreme Court on December 16, 1953. Expecting the opposition to question whether Congress had intended federal immunity to be binding on the states, Adams's attorneys presented the rather sordid history of the statute in question. At the heart of Adams's case was a law passed nearly a century earlier in response to a scandal in the House of Representatives. In 1857, two congressmen conceived a plot to sell their support for a piece of legislation being pushed by a group of lobbyists. To execute their plan, the lawmakers turned to a *New York Times* reporter for help. Unfortunately for them, word of their scheme leaked to other members of Congress. Outraged by the rumors, the House of Representatives established a special legislative committee to investigate. The committee summoned the *Times* journalist and ordered him to reveal the identities of the congressmen seeking the illegal payoff. The reporter refused to comply, and so the committee pushed to have him cited for contempt. However, the provision for contempt was deemed legally inadequate, spurring U.S. Rep. James L. Orr of South Carolina to draft new legislation that would govern congressional testimony. During the ensuing debate over the proposal, a Maryland congressman, Henry Winter Davis, neatly summarized the effect of the measure. "The purpose of the enactment is to grant [a witness] a pardon beforehand," Davis said. Passage will ensure that a witness will be "neither constrained here to give evidence against himself in a judicial proceeding in which he is defendant, nor to give evidence which may be used in any judicial proceeding which may hereafter be instituted. It is relieving him from prosecution, compelling him to testify — repealing the criminal law so far as he is concerned, and giving the investigations of this House free course."

Several lawmakers broached the matter of jurisdiction:

Would the states be required to recognize the federal grant of immunity or would they be free to prosecute based on the testimony? The record of their debate does not seem to include a definitive answer. Nevertheless, the House of Representatives passed the bill overwhelmingly, with only 12 members voting against it. The measure then headed to the Senate for consideration, where the federal-state question remerged. In opposing the bill, Senator George E. Pugh of Ohio wrote: "Congress can make no law to shield a witness from prosecution in the courts of the several States, nor prescribe any rule of evidence for those courts." Despite the fervor of his advocacy for states' rights, his argument elicited the support of few others. The Senate voted in favor of the law, 46 to 3. The statute was tweaked twice in subsequent years, first in 1859 and later in 1938. But in the 1953, the law remained fundamentally unchanged from its original form.

Adams's case hinged on just one sentence of the legislation: "No testimony given by a witness before either House, or before any Committee of either House, or before any Joint Committee established by a joint or concurrent resolution of the two Houses of Congress, shall be used as evidence in any criminal proceeding against him in any court, except in a prosecution for perjury in giving such testimony, but an official paper or record produced by him is not within the said privilege."

The language, while inelegant, appears unequivocal. "No [congressional] testimony ... shall be used as evidence in any criminal proceeding against [a witness] in any court ... ." The Adams legal team said the clarity of the law on this point powerfully refuted the argument by Maryland prosecutors. "The statute is not qualified in any respect. Therefore, if the statute is applicable, it can only mean that no testimony given before a congressional committee can be used as evidence against the witness in any criminal proceeding in any court. The word 'any' is all-inclusive," the lawyers wrote in their legal brief.

Adams's appeal also appeared to be bolstered by a recent federal court ruling right down the street from the Supreme Court. Less than a month after Maryland's high court upheld the conviction against Adams based on his Senate testimony, the Court of Appeals of the District of Columbia on July 2, 1953, issued a much different ruling in a similar case. In *Nelson v. United States*, Charles E. Nelson was prosecuted for gambling based in part on information he provided to the Senate. In reversing the man's conviction, the court succinctly captured the unfair and unconstitutional conundrum such congressional witnesses faced: "Nelson's freedom of choice had been dissolved in a brooding omnipresence of compulsion. The Committee threatened prosecution for contempt if he refused to answer, for perjury if he lied, and for gambling activities if he told the truth."

Concluding their case, Adams's lawyers went a step further. If the Supreme Court ruled in their favor, then the justices should prohibit Maryland prosecutors from taking yet another crack at convicting Adams. What appellate courts, including the Supreme Court, frequently do is resolve a specific legal dispute, such as the immunity question, and then remand the case back to the trial level court for a final ruling. But Adams's lawyers argued that the Supreme Court could — and should — end this case once and for all. If his congressional testimony should not have been admitted at criminal trial, then Adams should be cleared, they wrote. The only other substantive testimony proffered against Adams at trial was given by Maurice Jones. Jones's testimony, they continued, did nothing more than corroborate Adams's Senate testimony. Maryland prosecutors had said so themselves. If the Senate testimony had been properly barred at trial, there would have been nothing for Jones to corroborate. And under Maryland law, they wrote, "a defendant in a conspiracy case cannot be convicted on the uncorroborated testimony of an accomplice alone."

Not surprisingly, Maryland's highest-ranking prosecutors thought otherwise. In a terse legal brief submitted five days before oral arguments, Edward D. E. Rollins, Maryland's attorney general, J. Edgar Harvey, a deputy attorney general, and W. Giles Parker, assistant attorney general, attempted to eviscerate what they perceived as the wildly creative interpretation of law by the Adams legal team. Tackling the biggest constitutional issue first, the lawyers argued that Congress lacked the authority to set rules governing evidence in the courts of Maryland or any other state. "It is elementary that the States have the power to establish rules of practice and procedure in State courts. It is also true that questions involving the admissibility of evidence are to be governed by the law of the forum which, in the case at bar, was that of the State of Maryland," they wrote. Moreover, they continued: "It is to be presumed that when Congress employed the term 'in any Court,' the reference was to those courts over which Congress has traditionally had power." That is, federal courts.

If that argument didn't carry them to victory, then the state had another. Even if Congress intended immunity to extend to state courts, Adams failed to make use of the protection when he decided to give his testimony voluntarily. Citing the transcript of his testimony, prosecutors correctly pointed out that Adams had refused to answer certain questions by invoking the Fifth Amendment, while agreeing to answer other questions freely. This was a conclusive indication that Adams understood the legal rules. Adams also knew that the Senate committee lacked the legal power to compel him to answer. Senator Hunt explained this to Adams on the day he testified. "It cannot be disputed that [Adams] did have the right to refuse to testify upon the grounds of self-incrimination if he chose to avail himself of that privilege, and it is respectfully urged that, having failed to do so, he has no right to object to the use of such testimony against him in a proper case in a State court, and in the absence of a complete immunity granted by the statute, the evidence was properly admitted," they argued.

Prosecutors also took issue with how Adams's team relied on the recent District of Columbia court ruling for legal precedent. The two cases are different. Nelson was at risk of prosecution for contempt, they said. Adams was not. Adams's "testimony was freely, voluntarily and even eagerly given, and in view of the fact that he was accompanied by counsel, it is almost impossible to believe that he was not advised of his constitutional right to refuse to testify if he so desired."

If the state of Maryland prevailed, Adams would spend

seven years in prison regretting his decision to share anything with the Senate special committee. Why had a man known for being laconic and discrete divulged so much, or anything?

While the nation waited anxiously for the Supreme Court to rule in the school desegregation case, *Brown v. Board of Education*, Adams and his wife, Victorine, were preoccupied with the outcome of their own case. One month passed following oral arguments, and then a second. Meanwhile, the federal government continued to pursue Adams on another front, demanding roughly $800,000 for unpaid taxes. The confluence of events had the potential to leave Victorine without her husband, without her husband's earning power, and without a very considerable sum of money. To pay the government, Adams might be forced to liquidate his financial position in any number of companies, including the Charm Center, Baltimore's only black-owned and operated clothing retailer for women. Because segregation and racism restricted the shopping options for black women across the country, the Charm Center had become a popular spot for Baltimoreans, as well as out-of-towners. Even black celebrities such as Ella Fitzgerald would shop at the store when she was in Baltimore to give a performance on Pennsylvania Avenue. Not only would the Negro community as a whole suffer, so would the Adamses. Victorine retired from school teaching a few years earlier and went to work at the Charm Center, which served as an unofficial meeting place for her growing organization of politically active black women. There could be no doubt, their lives would be changed if the Supreme Court upheld the conviction and the IRS collected on its claim. And the colored community at large would also pay. So many of the best colored entertainment venues were owned or backed by Adams. And so many aspiring entrepreneurs would lose the single source of financing available to them.

On March 8, 1954, the Supreme Court rendered its decision in *Adams v. Maryland*, nearly five years after the 1949 raid that ultimately led to his appearance before the Senate special committee and more than a dozen Maryland judges. The majority opinion, written by Justice Hugo Black, a former member of the Ku Klux Klan, was less than three pages long, a length that seemed unlikely to accommodate a complex ruling overturning several Maryland courts and clarifying a major point of law. That would certainly require more words, more pages. Black first addressed the question of whether Adams's testimony was volunteered or delivered under threat of punishment. Clearly, Black opined, Adams would have been fined and possibly even sent to jail if he had refused to appear before the Senate committee. However, the court agreed with prosecutors on another key point. "It is true that Adams did not attempt to escape answering these questions by claiming a constitutional privilege to refuse to incriminate himself." But in the end, Adams's decision to expatiate so freely about the numbers in response to several questions did not matter, Black said. The relevant law does not require a person to plead the Fifth Amendment in order to "feel secure that his testimony will not be used to convict him of crime."

Adams had cleared one legal hurdle, but another remained, and it was the bigger of the two: does federal immunity protect witnesses from prosecution at the state and local levels? Just as Adams's lawyers had done in their brief, Black quoted the key sentence from the statute. "The Act forbids use of such evidence 'in any criminal proceeding ... in any court,'" Black wrote, adding: "Language could be no plainer." The court said the history surrounding the passage of the original bill in 1857 tended "to indicate that Congress was well aware that an ordinary person would read the phrase 'in any court' to include state courts. To construe this phrase as having any other meaning would make the Act a trap for the unwary."

The Supreme Court voted unanimously, 9-0, that the state of Maryland should not have been permitted to use Senate testimony against Adams. Two justices, Felix Frankfurter and Robert H. Jackson, concurred with the result, but on slightly different grounds. Jackson, for instance, used his concurrence to express his exasperation with what Adams was forced to endure. "The statute seems as unambiguous as language can be. If words mean anything, the statute extends its protection to all witnesses, to all testimony, and in all courts," Jackson wrote.

Despite the clear and even fervid language of the ruling in his favor, the Supreme Court decision was not a complete success for Adams. The court declined to prohibit Maryland prosecutors from taking Adams back to trial, remanding his case for further proceedings "not inconsistent with this opinion." Jackson went further in his concurrence, writing that Maryland retains "complete freedom to prosecute — she just has to work up her own evidence and cannot use that worked up by Congress."

In an editorial, the *Washington Post* hailed the Supreme

Court's ruling in Adams's case, explaining that the decision "has substantially enhanced the protection of witnesses before congressional committees." Perhaps because his fate was still uncertain, Adams expressed no emotion when he received word of the Supreme Court's ruling. While his wife wept, Adams impassively lit a cigar. Years later, Adams confessed that the Supreme Court decision pleased him. But the joy was not enough to overcome the years of frustration and anger he felt as a result of the state's relentless pursuit of him.

It was now up to the Baltimore state's attorney to decide whether to fight on, to make another attempt to put behind bars a man he considered to be one of the city's most notorious public enemies. Was another trial the right thing to do? Could he win, or would he just be wasting the public's money? Unable to use the Senate testimony, Sodaro decided to file a nolle prosequi motion, resting the state's case against Adams for good.

But the good news didn't free Adams's mind entirely. His battle with the federal government over unpaid taxes continued. During the eight months that followed the Supreme Court decision, his lawyers wrangled with the feds, working to reduce the amount owed. Finally, in *the* fall of 1954, he and the government struck a deal. He paid approximately $43,000 to settle the case. The year 1954 proved to be one of the most important in Adams's life. The ominous prospect of imprisonment had finally lifted, freeing him to focus on business and other interests. By now, Adams was meeting daily with a dozen or so different people seeking loans and business advice. But Baltimore police and prosecutors were not finished with Adams.

021 SEEKING POLITICAL EMPOWERMENT

By 1954, Baltimore's black community had notched a handful of civil rights victories. Johns Hopkins Hospital, the world-renowned medical institution located in the heart of East Baltimore, had hired its first Negro physician, Dr. Ralph J. Young. In 1952, Mayor Thomas D'Alesandro Jr. officially recognized racism as an actual problem in Baltimore by establishing a seven-member commission to investigate and make recommendations. In 1953, Baltimore's fire department halted its 95-year run as an all-white organization by hiring 10 Negroes, and the Lyric Opera House, the city's premier music venue, lifted its prohibition against black performers, opening its stage to the great vocalist Marian Anderson. And following the Supreme Court's 1954 school desegregation decision, Baltimore moved as quickly as any city in the nation to integrate. The one minor campaign to disrupt the integration effort in Baltimore, led by Bryant Bowles, president of a group he called the National Association for the Advancement of White People, proved unsuccessful, and there were no reports of violence or injuries, as there were in countless cities, particularly those in the south.

But the breakthroughs weren't having much, if any, impact on the lives of the overwhelming majority of Baltimore Negroes. In fact, when it came to employment, black Baltimoreans made nearly none of the professional progress that many expected during and following World War II. Before the United States entered the war, 2 percent of Baltimore's Negroes held managerial or supervisory positions. By 1954, that percentage stood at 2.3 percent. During that same 13-year span, blacks remained mired in back-breaking, low-paying labor jobs, with the percentage dipping only slightly from 58.2 percent before the war to 53.2 percent in 1954. The promise of the Great Migration appeared to be dissipating. For his part, Adams didn't grow discouraged, but he did recognize the need for a strategic shift to produce the change for which he longed. Providing financing one person at a time wasn't going to create citywide parity with whites, at least not in a timeframe he considered acceptable. So he reluctantly decided to invest more time and money in a venture with the potential to bring about a systemic transformation.

Adams first dipped into politics in 1946, brought along by his wife, Victorine, who plunged in by quitting her job and launching a major campaign to empower blacks through the ballot box. Negroes could sit around and wait for racial enlightenment among white politicians, or they could go out and force whites to pay attention to their needs and wishes. By registering to vote, participating in elections, and casting ballots for the office seekers who supported them, they could effect change. But this wasn't happening. Many blacks feared that there would be repercussions if they took part in the political process. Election places that drew black voters were closely monitored, often by men with baleful expressions and billy clubs. If a physical assault wasn't enough of a deterrent, blacks also ran the risk of being fired from their jobs and evicted from their homes. An unhappy white job supervisor could express his opposition by suddenly finding fault with the performance of his black employee. Likewise white landlords. Apathy and hopelessness were also disincentives. Why should a Negro bother to vote in hopes of more equitable treatment at a time when Congress couldn't even bring itself to pass anti-lynching legislation? There were also efforts to give blacks something more enjoyable to do on election day. Prominent blacks, allied with and financed by white bosses, would throw picnics, enticing guests with free food and alcohol to divert them from voting. Finally, there were logistical issues. Few blacks had vehicles of their own, and round-trip bus fare to the courthouse to register often came at the cost of more immediate needs. So in 1946, Victorine took the unprecedented step of creating the first formal political organization for black women in the city or state, the Colored Women's Democratic Campaign Committee of Maryland. Victorine and her colleagues were indefatigable and creative in their efforts to sign up voters, holding rallies, going door to door, and spreading the word one person at a time. While Victorine was enthusiastic, her husband was anything but. He was deeply ambivalent about the power of politics and politicians. If they had so much authority, why did they always turn to business people for help come election time? To his thinking, politicians couldn't exist without business people, but business people, particularly black business people, could easily do without politicians. That's not to say he was opposed; he was just unconvinced. Nevertheless, he played an important, but behind-the-scenes, role in his wife's registration drive, paying for buses to transport people from the West Baltimore gathering point, the all-black Douglass High School, to the downtown courthouse. William's cash and Victorine's determination generated a significant return. Roughly 9,000 people registered to vote as part of what would prove to be just the first in a series of Victorine-led efforts to increase black involvement and improve black Baltimore. Perhaps even more important, Victorine's effort spurred a generation of black Baltimoreans into political motion.

By 1954, reality had razed William Adams's ambivalence about the importance of politics and replaced it with fervor to identify and elect qualified black candidates. Black businessmen couldn't transform society on their own. "Without representation," he later conceded, "we were nowhere." But without Adams, even the ablest of black candidates were very nearly nowhere. Campaigns cost money, and there weren't many people willing or able to financially support black aspirants. Adams was an exception. Committed to the idea that he never would have made his fortune without the support of his fellow Negroes, he once again took to heart his responsibility to reciprocate.

In the 1954 election, Adams threw his support to

Harry A. Cole, a man with a sterling career record and an ugly political track record. A Korean War veteran and the first black lawyer to work for Maryland's Attorney General's Office, Cole was coming off two dispiriting political defeats. In 1950, he lost his bid to join the Maryland state legislature's lower chamber, the House of Delegates. A year later, Cole ran again, this time for the legislature of Baltimore City, the City Council. Different office, same result. Even so, Adams and Henry Parks liked and respected Cole and hired him to serve as the first lawyer for Parks Inc. But Cole still had his sights on politics and decided to run for yet another political office in 1954: a seat in the Maryland's state senate. Once again, his path to history, to becoming the first black member of the state legislature, was blocked by the seemingly insuperable political machine boss James H. "Jack" Pollack, a man who had been arrested more than a dozen times for everything from assault to murder and yet had mysteriously never been convicted of a serious crime, a surprising fact that strongly suggested that he had earned, or more likely bought, the loyalties of men in the criminal justice system. Wealth and determination aside, Adams was still very much a political novice. He and Cole seemed to be little match for Pollack and his beneficiary, incumbent state Sen. Bernard S. Melnicove. Moreover, Adams and Cole had to somehow reconcile their politics before forging an alliance. Like the majority of Negroes at the time, Cole was a Republican, the party of Abraham Lincoln, the great emancipator. But Adams was a Democrat, having been won over, like a growing segment of the black community, by the new era of progressive politics ushered in by Franklin Delano

Roosevelt. In the end, the two were able to bridge their ideological divide. Adams's devotion to a political party placed a distant second to his commitment to pragmatism. Pollack and his proxies were invariably Democrats, and the majority of black voters were squarely Republican, and so Adams enlisted without so much as requesting a future concession or favor. With no legal requirement to disclose political contributions and no incentive to volunteer such information, Adams personally contributed or raised all of Cole's campaign cash. He also provided Cole with a public address system, courtesy of his jukebox company, Biddison. Cole prevailed in his third attempt, narrowly defeating Melnicove by 37 votes. Cole could be forgiven for his acerbic post-election comments regarding the political boss. "For years, whenever a qualified candidate of color has campaigned against his ticket, [Mr. Pollack] has attempted to promote the idea that the candidate runs on the basis of race rather than one of qualifications to serve," Cole said at time of his election. For her part, Victorine Adams viewed Cole's victory as something exponentially more significant than the defeat of a Baltimore machine boss. "Harry Cole opened the floodgates because his victory proved we could do it," she said years later.

022 PLANTING SEEDS AND EVIDENCE

Adams kept his promise to Henry Parks, providing him with discrete financial support and absolute autonomy to operate the business. And Parks rewarded Adams's loyalty with steady financial growth and a rapid march to prominence. In the span of just three years, Parks transformed a two-person startup located in the back of a Baltimore warehouse into a national sponsor of the 1954 National League playoff series between the Brooklyn Dodgers and the New York Giants. For the occasion, Parks served up an advertising campaign that would prove to be one of the more memorable in marketing history. "More Parks sausages mom, please," a young boy pled again and again over the radio airwaves. Consumers were at least partially deceived by the ads; the boy's voice was actually provided by a grown woman. But the success of Parks did not sate Adams's entrepreneurial appetite. He yearned to create and cultivate more business triumphs, an ambition that had as much to do with the advancement of his fellow

169

Negroes as it did with profits. The best path to progress, he believed, passed directly through the legitimate business world. Investments and companies sometimes failed, but his faith in the transformative capacity of business ownership never did. In one effort, he launched a manufacturing company, Aerosol International Inc., in Baltimore's Brooklyn neighborhood to produce, among other offerings, a spray designed to stimulate plant growth. One 12-ounce can, the company vowed in an ad, would help as many as 600 plants to bloom bigger and more often, all for the price of just $1.98. Unfortunately, the firm itself did not flourish as expected. As he did so often throughout his career, Adams turned to a trusted long-time friend for assistance, bringing on Algernon Presswidge to run the operation. The company hadn't been managed or advertised adequately, he felt, and new leadership and some more patience would make a difference. Meanwhile, Adams was exhausting the patience of yet another Baltimore City Police Commissioner.

Shortly after his appointment as top cop, James M. Hepbron established a new unit dedicated exclusively to breaking up rackets and taking down gangsters, sending an unmistakable message about his priorities. So when he received a tip in 1957 that Little Willie and a close associate, Charles "The Fox" Burns, were brazenly operating an illegal gambling ring directly behind a city police station, Hepbron pounced, ordering a raid. His information, however, proved erroneous or out of date. Police found no one at the location and therefore orchestrated a second raid, this one on the home of Burns. On May 1, 1957, a law enforcement team that included the head of Hepbron's rackets division burst into Burns's apartment overlooking Druid Hill Park. Inside, they found Burns, Henry Parks, and two women watching a championship boxing match on television. Police arrested them all. They also apprehended Philip Taylor, who entered the apartment after the police arrived and tried to dump numbers paraphernalia when he saw them. Authorities quickly dropped the cases against Parks and the two women. But they proceeded against Burns and Taylor, charging them with conspiring to violate state gambling laws. Burns, a well-known Adams associate with a 1951 gambling conviction on his record, vehemently protested. The police planted the evidence, a collection of numbers slips, in his apartment, he claimed, adding that he had retired from the racket and gone into legal business. He now operated a 320-acre farm, he said. But the Morgan State University graduate and football star failed to convince the jury of his innocence. He received his second numbers conviction and a two-year prison sentence. Also found guilty, Taylor received a fine rather than jail time.

Burns refused to relent. Nor did he abandon his already unsuccessful argument that dirty cops framed him. Instead of taking an alternative legal approach, he muscled ahead, asserting in his bid for a new trial that the police who conducted the raid belonged behind bars, not him. The allegation, in this instance, approached absurdity. Yes, cops had been proven guilty time and again in Baltimore for illegal involvement in the numbers. But the crew that took down Burns didn't consist entirely of lower paid street cops more susceptible to breaking the rules to supplement their incomes. Two of the highest ranking officials in the department — Captain Hyman Goldstein and the head of the Rackets Division himself, Inspector Clarence O. Forrester — personally planned and presided over the raid. If Burns was accurate, then Goldstein and Forrester were likely aware of what transpired. At worst, they ordered the plant. Despite the apparent implausibility of the claim, the Maryland State Police launched an investigation of their own. During the course of the probe, one of the police officers who participated in the raid, Sergeant Charles Gross, committed suicide, slashing his own wrists. For the Baltimore Police Department, the dolorous situation was about to deteriorate further.

In response to Burns's habeas corpus motion contending that police planted the incriminating evidence that led to his conviction, Judge Michael J. Manley threw out the guilty verdict. Next, prosecutors charged Goldstein and Forrester, alleging that they lied about evidence in the Burns case, forced Philip Taylor into the apartment the day of the raid, and falsely accused him of illegal gambling. The ensuing trial proved even more sensational than the preceding events. First, someone attempted to illegally influence jurors by calling them at home, forcing the presiding judge to delay the start. Finally underway, the trial featured officers implicating their top commanders. Two members of the rackets unit testified that Goldstein instructed them to lie under oath to secure the convictions of Burns and Taylor. What's more, Goldstein provided them with numbers paraphernalia to list as evidence in the cases, they stated. Prosecutors concluded that the evidence clearly demonstrated Goldstein and Forrester's determination to take down an Adams lieutenant, regardless of the legality of their tactics. Max Sokol, a defense lawyer, shot back that state prosecutors not only were undoing good police work. They were actually promoting Adams and his syndicate. If there is a conviction in this case, he declaimed, "every dive will celebrate the conviction of Forrester and Goldstein. There will be more drinking this Saturday night than we ever had in the city of Baltimore. Little Willie and his cohorts and all the Block will celebrate." Not finished, Sokol asserted: "The city has now been taken over by the underworld. They have taken these men out of circulation and let the rackets run wild. They let Willie Adams run the city."

The sequestered jury of six men and six women completed their deliberations on Saturday, June 14, 1958, and rendered their verdict a 7:13 p.m.: Guilty. Forrester and Goldstein induced two subordinate officers to give perjured testimony, they concluded, completely vindicating Burns and Taylor in the process. For Forrester, the conviction would not stand. He secured a reversal, and prosecutors declined to retry the case against him. But they didn't allow him to walk free. One year later, in 1959, Forrester and Goldstein picked up additional convictions for their involvement with a 19-year-old prostitute. Forrester received an 18-month prison sentence, while Goldstein collected a total of three years for the two crimes.

Unknown is why police did not try to ensnare Henry Parks in their numbers scheme. It certainly wasn't for lack of opportunity or institutional support. Commissioner Hepbron himself asked Forrester and Goldstein to try to reopen the case against Parks after the dismissal. They declined.

Also unknown is the source of Commissioner

Hepbron's tip that Adams and Burns were running a racket in 1957. One possibility among many is Jack Pollack, the old political boss whom Adams defeated by proxy at the polls in the 1954 election. Perhaps he wanted to remove Adams from the political landscape heading into the 1958 races. Regardless, Pollack, a boxer in his youth, was spoiling for a rematch. He devised a strategy to better combat his new and surprisingly formidable opponent. Times were changing. Regardless of what his own personal feelings were regarding Negroes, if the public wanted black candidates, then that's what he would give them. After all, the people he put up for office were of secondary importance, the mere means to perpetuate his patronage-fueled power.

In 1958, Pollack backed a black candidate, Alvin Jones, to try to recapture the state Senate seat that Harry Cole, Adams's choice, seized the previous election cycle. Pollack succeeded. Jones defeated the incumbent by 2,000 votes, a wider margin than Cole enjoyed four years earlier. The old days of Pollack's boys doing the boss's bidding in the chambers of political power seemed to be new again.

Meanwhile, Adams's political success appeared to be an anomaly. Steep to begin with, the odds that Adams would emerge as a political kingmaker powerful enough to regularly deliver black candidates attentive to the needs of the black community suddenly looked less promising. But with characteristic stoicism, Adams viewed the situation differently. Setbacks were an inescapable part of business, something to be learned from and forgotten like a missed putt. A crisis of confidence would do nothing but serve as a foundation for future failure. He didn't lament the defeat.

Instead, he did what he had always done. He went back to work: In politics, devising a new strategy to defeat Pollack; in business, working to expand his real estate company, support Parks, and identify individuals worthy of financial backing; and in golf, playing as many holes as possible and traveling to compete in tournaments around the country. Indeed, 1958 wasn't a complete loss. Shortly before the fall election, he nearly won the Sixth City amateur golf championship in Ohio, missing out on the first-place trophy by just two strokes by shooting 75, 79, and 75 in the three-round tournament.

Likewise, Harry Cole pushed ahead. Undeterred by three defeats, he ran the following year, in 1959, for the Baltimore City Council. For his effort he picked up a fourth political loss. But this time around, Cole did not enjoy Adams's support. While in office, Cole intentionally failed to hold up his end of their relationship. Adams didn't demand special favors from the people he supported for political office. Instead, he generally expected one of two things in exchange for his financial support. One: They were to hire the people Adams recommended for the government jobs under their auspices. And two: they should grant him an open mind when he needed government support for a business enterprise.

Cole breached the agreement by awarding a liquor board inspector's job to the "wrong person," Adams learned after the fact. Adams did not seek retribution. He didn't operate that way, preferring instead to simply stop doing business with beneficiaries who betrayed him. Cole would be neither the last nor the most prominent politician to turn on Adams after receiving his backing.

023 THE BACKER GETS IT

By the time of Maryland's next statewide election, in 1962, the political tide had changed direction. After eight years of Republican rule, the Democrats recaptured the White House in 1960. What's more, the new president, John F. Kennedy, captured the nation's imagination in a way that his recent predecessors had not. With Kennedy at the helm, the disenfranchised had hope that a more civil and just day was about to dawn. In Baltimore, Adams could justly feel that the nation, particularly the black community, had come around to his way of thinking. The devotion to the party of Lincoln had diminished. The transition had come later than it should have, to Adams's thinking. If the black community had thrown its support to Democrats sooner, the civil rights movement might have made more progress. But Adams didn't indulge in hypothesizing about what might have been and wishing things were different. Rather, he dedicated his time to work, to doing what it took to bring about change.

In the race for State Senator in Baltimore's 4th

legislative district, Adams backed Verda Welcome, despite the fact that not a single state in the union had elected a black female state senator. A native North Carolinian like Adams, Welcome migrated to Baltimore in 1929, just as Adams had. She also shared Adams's dedication to improving the lives of black Baltimoreans. For example, she teamed up with Lillie May Jackson to fight the proliferation of liquor stores, which she considered predators in the black community. Unlike Adams, Welcome had completed her formal education, having attended Coppin Normal School and Morgan State University before going on to become a school teacher.

With the strong support of both William and Victorine Adams, Welcome triumphed over Jack Pollack's candidate. But neither Welcome nor Adams was ready to revel in their victory against the wily old political boss. Time and time again, Pollack had pulled off the improbable. Adams had seen this first hand when Pollack reclaimed the Senate seat with the audacious act of backing a Negro candidate. Recognizing the importance of organization and unity, Welcome and Adams established a group, the Fourth District Democratic Organization, with the dual objectives of backing black candidates and beating Pollack in future elections. However, the promising relationship between Adams and Welcome quickly deteriorated. According to one theory, Welcome intentionally distanced herself from Adams, not wanting to be so closely associated with his criminal brand now that she held office. In fact, a number of beneficiaries turned on Adams after parlaying his support into success, said Ethel Rich, a political activist with close ties to Adams's wife, Victorine. The people Adams backed frequently backed away from him as they grew successful, not wanting to be linked with "dirty money," she nearly hissed during an interview some 40 years after they first met.

Said Adams: "After Verda was elected to the Senate, she wasn't easy to work with. We didn't see eye to eye concerning politics."

President Lyndon B. Johnson appeared to have no such reservations about Adams, inviting him and his wife to a White House gala to celebrate their contribution to organizing and mobilizing black voters. While they gratefully accepted, William was coming to a disconcerting realization about President Johnson's successful fight for passage of the Civil Rights Act of 1964, landmark legislation that at long last outlawed discrimination and segregation. No longer would the force of law relegate Negroes to establishments designated as colored. Ninety-nine years after Lincoln issued the Emancipation Proclamation, Negroes could finally exercise their freedom and experience the many things they'd so long been denied. And although it required courage, for some racists weren't the least bit inhibited by the new legislation, the black community exercised their new freedom in droves. But ironically, in the heart of Adams, a man who had devoted so much to the empowerment of blacks, Johnson's historic handiwork sparked a profound ambivalence that would silently smolder for a lifetime.

Of course Adams wanted the black community to have access to opportunities and institutions equal to those enjoyed by whites. He'd personally invested heavily and, in many cases, unprofitably to fulfill his aspiration. But at the same time, he lamented the byproduct of integration — the unraveling of an artificially tight-knit black community. To be sure, the dispersal cost him financially. He had built and owned much of the parallel black social universe. He invested in or owned a number of venues lining his beloved Pennsylvania Avenue, and he developed the nationally recognized beach and live-music destination, Carr's Beach. When Negro customers branched out, Adams's revenues declined. But money was the least of his concerns. What he missed much more was the social aspect. Segregation had kept black people together. If you didn't run into someone you wanted to see on Pennsylvania Avenue during the 1940s and 1950s, then that person wasn't out for the evening. But with the Civil Rights Act, people dispersed. But characteristically, Adams responded by investing to make his nightclubs even nicer, to give blacks reason to forgo new-to-them offerings and return.

Former congressman and president of the NAACP Kweisi Mfume lyrically captured the heyday of Pennsylvania Avenue in his autobiography, *No Free Ride.* "I was mesmerized by its fast, brazen rhythms, its neon lights and fancy cars … . The black people here were as classy as any whites I'd seen … they drove in fancy fish-tail Cadillacs and handed them over to red-capped valets. The men stepped out sporting black Stetson hats, tailored sharkskin suits, bright silk ties and shoes so shiny you could see your face in them."

Already in steep decline, Pennsylvania Avenue was further ravaged during the riots that followed the assassination of Martin Luther King Jr. in April 1968. Fifty-four American cities suffered significant property damage during the week-long national nightmare. Baltimore was especially hard hit, with property damage valued at $12 million. Only Washington, D.C., incurred worse at $15 million. The damage wasn't exclusive to Pennsylvania Avenue. In fact, the first disturbance in Baltimore erupted on the city's east side. But eventually the rioting spread to the strip. It grew so intense there that police attempted to close the avenue from the 1700 block down to the 1500 block. The effort proved futile, as looters engulfed the entire length of the Pennsylvania Avenue commercial corridor. Forty-three people lost their lives in Baltimore, and 3,500 were injured.

Adams suffered no greater disappointment in his life than the demise of Pennsylvania Avenue, according to friends. And for good reason. So brisk was the business in illegal narcotics along The Avenue that the Baltimore Police Department assigned eight undercover agents to work the strip around the clock. The area's population plunged 20 percent between 1950 and 1960, nearly a decade before the riots, and the assessed value of land plummeted by 10.8 percent between 1953 and 1963.

Even three decades after the riots, after the complete collapse of Pennsylvania Avenue due in large part to the rise of drugs, Adams still held hope that he and others could restore the Gold Coast to its former glory, although he made public comments to the contrary. "Those days are gone forever. It'll never be The Avenue it was between 1935 and the early 50s," he told a newspaper reporter.

"He's tried to hold on. It's a lost cause, and he still doesn't want to give it up," said Terry Prestwidge, wife of Adams's first numbers lieutenant and his first Club Casino partner, Algernon.

Unrelenting, Adams also continued the initiative to identify and support black candidates for political office and other important government positions. For three of his next success stories he didn't have to look far. In 1963, he backed Henry Parks for a seat on the Baltimore City Council. Parks, Adams later conceded, didn't need much of his help. Parks had already emerged as a star in political circles, despite his heavy workload at Parks Sausage. In 1966, Adams's wife, Victorine, ran for and won a seat in the state's House of Delegates. A year later, she, too, successfully ran for Baltimore City Council, becoming the first black woman in the city's nearly 200-year history to serve on Baltimore's legislature. She also broke the glass ceiling. Although four women had served before her, none had won election. All four were appointed to complete the terms of their husbands.

But both Parks and Adams encountered political turbulence along the way. During his tenure as a Baltimore City councilman, Parks championed initiatives designed to promote equity and economic development for the black community. But just as often as he fought for these measures, the majority of the city's legislature fought back, thwarting him time after time. Nevertheless, he continued to toil for what he believed in until the city's Board of Ethics blocked his plan to invest in a major new real estate venture in Baltimore's Inner Harbor, citing a conflict of interest. Rather than accept the ruling, Parks resigned from the City Council. .

Days later, Parks also relinquished his chairmanship of the powerful Fourth District Democratic Organization, frustrated by his inability to get members to fall in line and do what he considered right. The most noxious offender, to his thinking, was state Senator Verda Welcome, whom Adams and Parks had helped to ensconce in the legislature in the first place. The ingratitude was one thing. But she was creating an unnecessary and potentially fatal fissure in their group, which Adams and Welcome had created in 1962. Parks groused that Welcome "was allowing petty conflicts to divide the organization." Similarly indignant, Welcome viewed Adams and Parks as the tail trying to wag the dog that she created on her own following her first election victory to the state's House of Delegates in 1958. Welcome discounted the role Adams played in defeating political boss Jack Pollack. He had helped, to be sure, but not until Welcome took over did they develop the power to prevail in election after election.

One state lawmaker, Lena K. Lee, went further in her assessment, claiming Parks and Adams had betrayed the true black power of Northwest Baltimore. Both men, she said, had been "invited into Senator Welcome's very own Fourth District political organization (and then) took it back from her and proceeded by back-room tricks to depose and destroy her." After vowing that he would never again support Welcome, Parks declined to attend the group's most important meeting of the year on the evening of November 17, 1969, where members were scheduled to select their candidates for the upcoming elections and leaders for their organization. The meeting sprawled to more than three hours in length, as members clashed about the future of their group and, by extension, black candidates. Although Adams shared Parks's thoughts about

Welcome and the direction she was taking the group, he wouldn't walk away out of pique. He didn't take the nasty business personally, and instead focused on how to improve the situation. He did so on this occasion by delivering an impassioned speech. Adams succeeded, becoming the only opponent of Welcome to win re-election to the club's board of directors. After the contentious meeting, Welcome, who herself won unanimous support for her re-election bid, shared her rather tepid support of Adams with a reporter: "He was very well-liked by the organization and made a good statement explaining that, primarily, he was for the economic growth and development of the community, not for or against any particular persons."

Leaving the meeting, Adams said: "I gave a talk from my heart and head. Mrs. Welcome said some things about our public opposition to each other and I answered. My position is this: I'm not seeking political bossism, but I do want to see the black community gain as much economically as it has politically." Days later, one of the city's leading newspapers effectively scoffed at Adams. On the final day of the 1960s, *The Evening Sun* humorously captured just how powerful Adams had become. In a comic column, the paper made a series of predictions, including that Adams would be elected mayor of Baltimore in the upcoming 1971 election. "Why not?" the paper asked. "He already runs the damn town."

Around the same time, a competing newspaper referred to Adams as "the fabled phantom of the Fourth District," and declared that Adams "not only has driven Jack Pollack out of Negro territory but has replaced him as the district's unrivaled political power broker."

024 NEW BLOOD

Adams and Parks may have been scuffling in the political arena, but they were thriving in business. With Henry at the helm, Parks Inc. grew exponentially. Between 1966 and 1969, revenue surged by 50 percent from $6 million to $9 million. The time had come, Parks concluded, to take another bold step forward, this one without any precedent in corporate America. Parks decided to conduct an initial public offering, a move that, if successful, would make his company the first black-owned and operated enterprise to have its shares traded on Wall Street. With the quiet but constant support of Adams, Henry Parks was about to hurdle one the most significant color barriers in business. In the months before the IPO, Parks garnered national media attention, landing on the cover of *Business Week* magazine, among other outlets

"I think I've proven a point," Parks told the publication. "Negroes can not only be successful, but they can be successful on the same terms as anyone else."

Parks conceded, however, that his company faced certain obstacles as a result of race. For example, he said that he still struggled to attract experienced managers to his company. Many potential white applicants didn't seem interested in working for a black president, no matter how successful his company, and few Negroes had the experience to deliver what Parks Inc. needed.

In the early 1970s, Parks hired an outside firm to help him recruit the executive-level talent he needed to continue to expand his company. He tapped an outfit led by a newly minted graduate of the Harvard Business School, who in turn contacted one of his former Harvard classmates to gauge his interest in joining the meat company. None, said Theo C. Rodgers, a consultant who was searching for a manufacturing company to acquire and operate. His friend pleaded. Just go on an interview. Do it as a favor to me to show Parks that I represent high-caliber job candidates, he urged. Rodgers ultimately capitulated, rationalizing that at least it would give him the opportunity to meet one of the nation's top business leaders who was black.

Not needing or wanting a job, Rodgers struggled to suppress a certain sense of arrogance. He boldly told Parks that he'd only be interested if he were named assistant to the president, Parks himself, and given nearly unlimited latitude to participate in the leadership of the company — demands that were very unlikely to be granted to such a young person with no experience at the company. But Parks agreed to his demands, and Rodgers accepted, setting in motion a chain of events that would lead to one of the most important relationships of William Adams's life.

While Rodgers, then just 31 years old, may have been

relatively young for such a senior position with a publicly traded company, he had already put together an impressive resume. General Motors, then one of the world's leading companies, recruited Rodgers, a mechanical engineering major, right out of college, Tennessee State University, in 1964. Shortly thereafter, he joined a company on the cutting edge of innovation, Dow Corning, and from there he went on to the nation's leading MBA program at Harvard. Just as important as his experience and skills was his attitude about work. Before hiring Rodgers, Parks conducted a background check. Respondents told Parks that Rodgers was a Harvard MBA who didn't act like one, meaning he wasn't self-satisfied, he didn't feel entitled by his prestigious degree and always stood at the ready to do whatever heavy lifting was necessary. Rodgers was a generation younger than Adams and Parks, but they all had an entrepreneurial drive in common. Throughout their lives, they devised creative ways to make money and worked hard to earn it. Adams, for example, figured out as a small child in the 1920s how to maximize his revenue from picking cotton. Since pickers got paid by the weight of their day's harvest, Adams worked when the fields were heaviest with dew, a time when many others preferred to sleep. Not satisfied with his income, he taught himself how to repair and build bicycles. Leveraging that skill, he bought bikes in disrepair, ordered replacement parts from the Montgomery Ward catalogue, restored the bikes, and then sold them at a profit.

Rodgers, meanwhile, started out handling his uncle's newspaper route. He impressed the manager and earned his own route and, later, a management job at the distribution center, all before graduating from high school. While in college, he developed several money-making ventures, including one that turned segregation on its head. To get home during breaks from northern colleges, black students bound for the South had little choice but to take the segregated train. Rodgers decided to lease an entire train passenger car and sell tickets to students who liked the idea of riding in privacy where they could do what college students do — have fun — without having to worry about inciting a negative reaction from the conductor or white passengers. The train company was only too happy to get the black students out of sight, and Rodgers could make a profit by selling enough tickets to surpass the cost of the car.

Rodgers quickly earned the trust of Adams and Parks, who demonstrated their faith by giving him their most critical assignments, professional and personal. For example, they tapped him to acquire a hog slaughtering plant so that Parks Inc. could control the quality of its raw materials. When the slaughterhouse later faltered, losing as much as $15,000 a week and jeopardizing the company's future, Adams and Parks sent Rodgers to identify and fix the problem, which he did. And when a real estate venture started siphoning cash from their personal accounts, they put Rodgers on it.

But not everybody perfectly executed Adams's will.

Heading into the 1971 city election, Baltimore was just months away from a seismic demographic shift. The following year, the number of black residents would, for the first time, surpass the number of whites. To some, the time seemed right, at last, for Baltimore to elect its first black mayor. George Russell, a member of William Adams's inner circle, agreed, deciding to pursue the office himself, which created a conflict for Adams. When the two men first met in early 1950s, Russell instantly impressed Adams, much in the same way Henry Parks had. Highly intelligent and a law school graduate, Russell hustled indefatigably in pursuit of professional success. Constantly on the lookout for new business, Russell later joked that he would have passed his business card to a bride and groom on their wedding day in hopes of securing a new client. When Adams first hired Russell for a legal assignment, Russell responded by calling Adams at home at 7 a.m. to discuss the matter. Adams initially growled, asking his new lawyer why he was calling so early. But Adams ultimately appreciated the drive he demonstrated. Not long after, Adams turned over all of his private legal work to Russell. Adams and Parks also retained Russell to work for their sausage company, where he handled union negotiations and land acquisitions, among other assignments. Adams went even further on behalf of Russell.

In 1966, to express his gratitude to Adams for the critical votes he delivered for his hard-fought re-election campaign, Governor J. Milliard Tawes effectively gave a judgeship to Adams to fill. Adams asked Russell if he wanted it, and Russell accepted, becoming the first black in the state to serve as a judge on a court bench higher than the district level. Two years later, Russell made more history. The newly elected mayor of Baltimore, Thomas D'Alesandro III, grateful to Adams and Henry Parks for helping to push him to victory, sought their input on who he should appoint as the first black city solicitor. Adams again turned to Russell, but in this instance he needed to do a little lobbying first.

The undisputed white political kingmaker at the time, Irvin Kovens, had another person in mind for the post. Having known each other for 30 years, Adams and Kovens were personally and politically close, although they declined to publicly discuss the history of their relationship. When a reporter asked them about it, both men said: "Oh, it goes back to the early '30s," and they left it at that. By working in tandem, they were reconfiguring the political landscape as they saw fit. In this case, Kovens and Adams disagreed, but Adams eventually won him over. And so, in 1968, Russell became city solicitor, making him the city's top legal advisor. The next disagreement between Adams and Kovens regarding Russell produced a different result.

Three years later, when Mayor D'Alesandro made the surprising decision not to run for re-election, Russell made the equally surprising decision to seek the office. Russell's move, made without consulting Adams, threatened to crack the political alliance between Adams and Kovens. Kovens, a gregarious man with a fondness for long cigars, had already selected his horse for the upcoming election, City Council President William Donald Schaefer, and this time he would not acquiesce to an alternative. Adams had a decision to make: Break with his long-time friend and lawyer, George Russell, or with Kovens, who had worked so hard with Adams to make Baltimore a more equitable place for Negroes. The decision was further complicated by the fact that Kovens was, by this time, far more powerful than any elected official. By going with Russell, he might lose an irreplaceable partner. What's more, Adams felt Russell was not the right man for the job. That's not to say that Adams didn't believe in the business acumen and intelligence of his friend. He would later demonstrate his faith in Russell by entrusting him with his own freedom. But Adams didn't believe Russell was cut out for politics. Yes, he shared Russell's desire to see a black mayor, but Russell wasn't the one. Meanwhile, Kovens's candidate had privately vowed to represent whites and blacks alike if elected. Adams struck something of a compromise by backing Russell but also contributing to Schaefer's campaign.

Despite the entry of another black candidate, Clarence M. Mitchell III, Russell won 80 percent of the city's black vote. But it wasn't enough. Schaefer picked up 10 percent of the black vote and trounced Russell among whites. Schaefer didn't, however, dispense with his former opponent, deciding instead to invite Russell to remain on the Board of Estimates. In his 1971 bid for mayor, Russell proved to be way out in front of his fellow Baltimoreans. Not until 1987 would the city finally elect an African-American, becoming the very last major city with a majority black population to do so.

Nearly 40 years after his failed campaign for mayor, Russell conceded that it was "insane" for him to run and that he wasn't a particularly deft candidate. In other words, Adams had been correct. He had also been correct in maintaining that Russell should continue to practice law. Even into his 80s, Russell remained one of the most successful, prominent, and even revered attorneys in Baltimore.

Adams and Kovens, meanwhile, got back to work shaping the city and state.

025 EXECUTION DAY

Little Willie Adams will be among the next to die. So threatened an anonymous caller to a journalist at the *News American* newspaper in mid-July 1973. "We have five more executions set for this month," he said, providing the full list of targets. The man identified himself only as the No. 2 official at a group called Black October, instantly establishing the credibility of the threat. Just days earlier, the organization conducted two separate execution-style murders in Baltimore City, including one of a state lawmaker.

On July 13, one or more members of Baltimore October ambushed Maryland State Delegate James A. "Turk" Scott Jr. in the parking garage outside of his home, shooting him at least a dozen times in the chest and legs. The group did the same to George L. Evans directly in front of his house. Law authorities couldn't help but link the two murders. The killer or killers had surrounded the bodies of both victims with literature bearing Black

October's name and their motive: to eliminate individuals who were poisoning the black community with illegal drugs. The flyers at the Scott crime scene stated: "These persons are known drug dealers. Selling drugs is an act of treason. The penalty for treason is 'death'!!" The pamphlets surrounding Evans's corpse blared: "He too has paid the penalty for treason. There is no hope in dope. Off the pusher. Save black children." The killers took time to literally spread their message, but they didn't bother with the money in Evans's pocket: $65.

Both Scott and Evans had, in fact, been criminally charged by law enforcement for alleged involvement in drug distribution. Scott stood accused of smuggling $10 million of heroin into Baltimore. The murder obviously preempted his federal trial, which had been scheduled to start one month after the fatal attack. Likewise, Evans had been indicted on drug-related charges, but he escaped conviction.

Next to die, the caller told the reporter, are Samuel Kennedy, Frank Dintilli, "Pearl Street Reds," a woman identified only as Phyllis, and Little Willie Adams. Kennedy, an ex-cop suspected of stealing heroin from the Baltimore City Police Department, seemed to fit with Black October's agenda. But Adams, a man revered in black Baltimore? Accused of pushing drugs in the black community?

When informed of the threat made on his life, Adams was initially dismissive, saying he didn't even believe in the existence of Black October, a group claiming 30 black Vietnam veterans as members. "From all indications in the community, nobody has found a single source knowing a member of the group," he said, revealing that he was at least concerned enough to ask questions of his sprawling network of contacts. Adams also rejected Black October's implied assertion that he was somehow involved in the distribution of illegal narcotics. "I don't know why I'm on the list and I'll go about my business as usual," he said. But, in fact, Adams did not go on with business as usual. For the first time in a long time, he felt the need for protection.

Adams knew there were those who believed he had used his millions to enter the lucrative underworld businesses of prostitution and drugs. Some of those people, many of them dangerous, were convinced that he was cornering the drug market and effectively pre-empting their business. If that weren't enough, they thought, he was somehow able to preserve his noble public image while engaged in a decidedly ignoble business, one that was ravaging generations of young blacks, and for that they loathed and resented him. Adams vociferously denied any involvement in prostitution or drugs. When directly asked about the issue while making a presentation at Morgan State University, he declared: I do not have a penny in drugs. I am against drugs. I see every day what it does to our people, and I know what it will do down the years. I repeat, I have nothing to do with heroin or any other drugs."

In fact, he repeatedly expressed views similar to those of the Black October. Drugs were robbing the black community of its vitality, of its ability to make further progress, to build businesses, and to raise families. Adams had a front-row seat to the devastation perched in his second-floor office above the Club Casino on his beloved Pennsylvania Avenue. Where once the street teemed with thriving people it was now littered with sick individuals broken by addiction. Drugs, he lamented, were ruining Baltimore, particularly the black community. Despite the fervor and ostensible sincerity of his protestations, some remained incredulous, and not without reason. To start with, the business path from Prohibition-era alcohol distribution and illegal gambling to drug dealing and prostitution was well worn by kingpins such as Adams. Squeezed by the repeal of Prohibition and the proliferation of legal gambling venues and enticed by the enormously profitable drug trade, many diversified. The skeptics had seen it all before. What's more, Adams by now had forged associations, some tight, some considerably less so, with many hundreds of people in Baltimore through the numbers and other undertakings. Consider, for example, that one estimate pinned his numbers organization at roughly 1,000 people in 1949. It is all but inconceivable to believe that not one of them had at least dabbled in drugs or prostitution. Adams, himself, allowed that some people he had invested in during the years got involved in prostitution. They owned establishments where the oldest business clearly took place. Adams was the first one to confess that he had made scores of bad investments, but it now appeared, in light of the threat from Black October, that those mistakes might cost him more than money.

Fortunately for Adams and the four others on Black October's hit list, there would be no more bloodshed in the case. Law enforcement charged Sherman Dobson with the murder of Scott, having found his fingerprints on the flyers left at the murder scene, among other pieces of evidence. Nevertheless, a jury ultimately acquitted him.

While Adams escaped harm in 1973, the illegal

business that he practiced to establish the financial foundation for myriad future endeavors — the numbers — did not. In that same year, Maryland launched a state-sanctioned lottery, a game identical to the numbers save for the facts that it was now legal and the same government that relentlessly pursued Adams was now a banker. Unfortunately, the state proved less adept at the business than Adams. Just months after starting the lottery, Maryland started to resort to various gimmicks to boost sales, which were trailing projections by some 35 percent.

026 THE SALE AND THE START-UP

On Monday, Dec. 9, 1974, Henry Parks announced that his company had reached another milestone: its first dividend payout. During the 12-month period that closed at the end of September, Parks generated sales of $12.9 million and a profit of $319,933. "In taking this action," Parks said, "the board recognizes that the company has reached a level of financial maturity where a dividend payout will not jeopardize the firm's financial stability and means for expansion."

Adams, despite his many contributions, attributed the company's strength entirely to Henry Parks. "Mr. Parks and I discuss the problems of the company quite a bit — but I give him all of the credit for Parks Sausage being a successful company."

Parks held Adams in similarly high regard.

"Will is one of the better business minds you'll run across. He's operated a sound business in everything he's been in," Parks said. "We think quite a bit alike. That's what attracted me to Will in the first place. He has come up the hard way in the black community. He has made his money in various ways, and has constantly sought to improve himself. The penalty he's had to pay in terms of progress is that he had to be better than the next guy."

Parks also highly valued his assistant, Theo Rodgers, telling a journalist: "I expect him to run this business someday."

But while Henry Parks's company and relationships with were strong, his health was not. Suffering from Parkinson's disease, he decided a short time later to cash out of his company and step away. Word of Parks's illness and interest in selling reached Reginald F. Lewis, a young man in his early 30s who grew up not far from where Adams had rebuilt bicycles in East Baltimore generations earlier. Like Adams and Parks, Lewis also had dreams of business superstardom, and he appeared to be well on his way. A graduate of Harvard Law School, Lewis was a corporate lawyer on Wall Street where he worked for some of the nation's biggest corporations, including General Foods. He had no interest, however, in serving clients for the rest of his career. He wanted to build a company of his own capable of competing with the titans. In 1975, he made his first attempt to acquire another company: Parks Inc. Although the Baltimore firm had sold shares to the public six years earlier, Henry Parks and William Adams maintained a controlling stake in the company. Lewis reached out to a friend to arrange a meeting: Ellis Goodman, son-in-law of Irvin Kovens, the close personal and political ally of Adams and Parks. However, the two sides did not forge a deal. Of course, Lewis did ultimately achieve his goal. In 1983, he set up TLC Group and executed a $22.5 million leveraged buyout of McCall Pattern Co. After selling McCall at an enormous profit four years later, he engineered the largest offshore leveraged buyout by an American company up to that point, acquiring the international division of Beatrice Foods in a $985 million deal.

Two years later, in 1977, Parks agreed to sell his company to Norin Corp., a Miami-based holding firm, for $5.1 million in cash, or $10 a share. At the time of the sale, Adams owned 31 percent of Parks Inc., while company officers held roughly 32 percent. Norin retained Raymond Haysbert as chief executive. The company also pushed to keep Rodgers, but he decided to go in another direction with Adams.

As Rodgers finalized the sale of Parks to Norin, the prominent Baltimore newspaper columnist Michael Olesker identified William Adams as one of the five most powerful men in Baltimore, the city that was the locus of power for the entire state. "Publicly, his profile never has been more low-key," Olesker wrote. "Privately, he still has enormous power in politics, in business and in real estate, and he is close friends with the governor and the mayor. By far he is the most powerful black person in the city, despite holding no office. If he wants something done, it gets done."

Around the same time, Adams granted an illuminating interview to a tiny newspaper in the town of his youth, Zebulon, North Carolina. While many in Baltimore considered Adams a self-interested, self-promoting kingmaker, Adams revealed his true motivation. "I have liked working in politics. I know it's a need, and I am more interested now in getting people in the office who will understand the needs, instead of making headlines all the time," he told *The Zebulon Record*. "At first we had to get the doors open. The emphasis was getting any black in office. Now, the emphasis is getting the right black in office."

A short time later, Adams gave voice to his core beliefs while delivering the commencement speech at Morris Brown College in Atlanta. Exhorting the class of 1977 to work hard and persevere, Adams emphasized the importance of overcoming mistakes, of refusing to be derailed or discouraged by a misstep. With humility, he confessed to making a mistake or two, including one that probably lost him a substantial sum. In the 1960s, he revealed, an old friend named Irvin Kovens and a few others asked Adams to invest in a new project in Las Vegas, a hotel and casino to be named Caesar's Palace. Adams expressed interested but didn't, ultimately, join the partnership. Learn from your mistakes and move on, he said, but never forget the solemn obligation we each have to all of our fellow human beings. "Realize," he concluded, "the world does not owe you a living, but you owe it to the world to be productive."

Back in Baltimore, with their time at Parks Inc. drawing to a close, Adams pitched Rodgers on the idea of creating a real estate development company together. Adams's proposal appeared somewhat curious. A real estate company made sense for him, considering the holdings already in his portfolio. What didn't appear entirely logical was his choice of partner. Rodgers had no experience in real estate development. Not so much as a single class in college. But Adams believed devoutly in the notion that with intelligence and hard work a person could overcome inexperience and produce success. So he offered Rodgers his standard terms: you do the work, I'll provide the financing, and we'll split the profits 50-50. Rodgers drafted a business plan, and their new company was born in 1977, the "A" standing for Adams, the "R" for Rodgers. In keeping with Rodgers's business plan, A&R also stood in its early days for a commitment to minimizing market risk. The company focused exclusively on government contracts that weren't subject to the inevitable gyrations of the economy and housing prices. Perhaps less glamorous than developing architecturally iconic towers for big-name buyers able to pay big-time prices, A&R's work offered stability. This strategic decision proved prescient when the nation plunged into a fuel crisis and then the worst recession since the Great Depression. In 1980, interest rates soared to more than 21 percent, cruelly punishing the housing market.

A&R moved forward unscathed, pursuing and winning federal contracts. More specifically, A&R developed two types of government projects: turnkey and Section 8 housing. A turnkey project is one where a government entity decides to erect housing for the poor, the elderly, students, or the disabled and hires a developer to perform all of the work, from land acquisition to construction. The developer gets paid upon delivery of the completed building. Payment has no relationship to vacancy rates or rent amounts collected, two key sources of market-rate risk in private-sector development. Section 8 refers to the federal housing voucher program that provides rent subsidies to low-income people. In this type of deal, a developer secures a 20- to 30-year contract with the government to construct and operate a residential building for the poor. Market-rate risk is eliminated by the federal guarantee to cover the rent for every unit. A&R secured a number of these deals during its early days, including the $5.2 million Lakeview Towers project overlooking Druid Hill Park, Bradford House Apartments, a $3.9 million building on Maryland's Eastern Shore, and the Trinity House Apartments, a $3.7 million effort in Waynesboro, Pennsylvania. Success and a growing reputation threw open the door to additional opportunities, including one President Jimmy Carter urgently wanted completed.

The federal government's executive branch also took an interest in Adams's longtime friend and political ally, Irvin Kovens. In the summer of 1977, a federal jury convicted Kovens and four others for illegally paying Maryland's governor hundreds of thousands of dollars to exert his influence to bolster the value of a piece of real estate they owned. Kovens received a three-year prison sentence.

Adams the political kingmaker stood undiminished, a fact that inspired one citywide elected official, Comptroller Hyman Pressman, to pen a poem in the *Baltimore Afro-American* newspaper: "His power makes politicians quake/while jogging around Ashburton Lake./Candidates for mayor, you'll all look silly,/without the support of Little Willie."

027 THE WIRETAP

On the afternoon of Tuesday, September 25, 1979, Marvin Mandel, the recently deposed and disgraced governor of Maryland, placed a telephone call to Irvin Kovens, the man most responsible for Mandel's political ascent and at least partially responsible for his criminal fall. In the midst of a pitched legal battle to avoid prison following their convictions two years earlier, Mandel and Kovens had more than their share of trouble. Now, so did their dear friend and ally. The police are searching for Adams, Mandel said. They've already raided his home. The information surprised Kovens and with good reason. Kovens and Adams had just met, and Adams didn't say a word about any investigation.

A short time later, Adams's long-time friend and business partner, Henry Parks, turned his television set on and flipped the channel to the local news. He couldn't believe what he saw and heard. He wouldn't. The news anchor reported that William Adams, now in his mid-60s, was in police custody, accused of leading a $5 million gambling ring. Adams had been picked up along with 36 others during a sweep that included 51 simultaneous raids. A reporter for the Baltimore *Afro-American* newspaper called Parks in hopes of getting his reaction to the astonishing news. "How am I supposed to react?" Parks barked. "Here is a man I know like the back of my hand, and they are telling us he's a criminal? I don't believe one minute of what I heard."

Such incredulity and outrage spread far and fast.

"I don't understand it. It's got to be some kind of vendetta," Charles Burns, a former numbers operator and Adams associate, said. "It just seems crazy to me."

"I can't believe it. He would have to tell me himself, that's the only way I would believe it," said Lloyal Randolph, a former state lawmaker and a long-time political ally of Adams.

In fact, Adams's arrest came as a surprise even to law enforcement. The police received a tip about a West Baltimore numbers runner, William B. "Pie" Simpson, in the summer of 1979 and launched an investigation. They surveilled his home and secured permission to tap his phone. The telephone is what led to Adams.

"We had no intelligence [at the outset of the investigation] from any source that he [Mr. Adams] was involved," Floyd O. Pond, the assistant state's attorney who led the initiative, said. "We were stunned."

One law enforcement official involved in the investigation was anything but surprised. "Willie just couldn't keep his hands out of it," the individual, granted anonymity, told a reporter.

Adams himself didn't know about the investigation

until the police showed up at his house to arrest him, but he was well acquainted with the original target of the investigation. Simpson was his nephew, one of his sister Luvenia's three children. There was no disputing that two had talked on the telephone. But what, exactly, did they say? And would their words result in jail time?

Adams adamantly denied any involvement. "If I'm involved in a $5 million-a-year operation, I'd like to know where the money is," he bristled. "My name has been linked to many things before. But anytime you're politically involved you become a target. I'm absolutely innocent of any numbers charges."

Nevertheless, Adams once again needed a good lawyer. He turned naturally to George Russell, but some associates encouraged him to reconsider. The times are different, and you need an attorney with the same firepower that the city has already turned on you with this massive raid, they reasoned, recommending instead Arnold Weiner, who represented former Governor Mandel in his corruption trial. Adams hesitated, torn by his loyalty to Russell and the possibility that the advice he was receiving was correct. Ultimately and predictably, loyalty prevailed. He brought on Russell and co-counsel Kenneth L. Thompson to keep him out of prison.

The legal process started promisingly for Adams and Russell. The first charge against Adams was thrown out on grounds that a judge hadn't correctly completed the charging documents. But the prosecutors were not going down to defeat on a technicality. The next day, they leveled three new gambling charges against Adams. It appeared as if the State's Attorney's Office of Baltimore was calling for a rematch of their epic battle with Adams during the 1940s and '50s. And once again, Adams was up for the fight. He had no choice. The next round also went to Adams, as the state's intermediate appellate court, the Court of Special Appeals, knocked down the prosecutors' new charges, explaining that "the apparent circumstances surrounding the enhanced charges gave rise to a genuine risk of retaliation." But the Court of Special Appeals' ruling wouldn't stand forever, although it almost certainly felt that way to the participants. Not until three years after Adams's 1979 arrest did the state's highest court, the Court of Appeals, weigh in, ruling that the charges were in fact valid and that the case against Adams could and should proceed. "Adams has not presented any objective evidence of bad faith on the part of [prosecutors]," Chief Judge Robert C. Murphy wrote in a unanimous decision, adding that Adams's "subjective fears, standing alone" do not warrant the dismissal of the case. Not participating in the case was Judge Harry Cole, the man who Adams first backed for political office in 1954 and who now had no choice but to recuse himself. In fact, recusals came pouring in. A total of 10 judges excused themselves from *State of Maryland v. Adams*, citing personal and political relationships with the defendant.

Finally, in 1984, Adams, now 70 years old, got his day in court. But unfortunately for him, the prosecutors by now had considerable experience not only trying cases stemming from the 1979 raid, but also winning them. Of the 37 people arrested, 36 had been tried and 32 of them convicted. Only Adams's case remained. On Monday, June 2, in Baltimore City Circuit Court, prosecutors opened their case against Adams, hoping to improve their record to 33 out of 37 and, more importantly, to put Baltimore's kingpin behind bars once and for all.

The state's case against Adams relied heavily on the wiretapped phone conversations, more than 60 in all. The most important of these recorded discussions were between Adams and Simpson, who had already been convicted of 10 counts of illegal gambling and sentenced to five years in prison, all suspended, and fined $10,000. However, the state did not accept that Simpson served as the mastermind of the illegal gambling network. That distinction belonged to Adams, prosecutors believed. Adams's continued participation in numbers at the very highest level would be established, along with his guilt, during 10 phone calls the state had secretly recorded between Adams and Simpson, they maintained. Their conversation of August 29, 1979, was typical of most of the others. They talked business. During this particular discussion, Adams upbraided his nephew for his sloppy practices and resulting money problems. While neither man referred explicitly to the nature of their business, the state asserted that the subject of their conversation was clear, although implied: illegal gambling. Nine of the 10 calls were similarly suggestive. They talked about business, but never introduced a single detail about the kind of operation under discussion. For instance, in one exchange, Adams told Simpson that he was "overpaying" and therefore unlikely to "wind up with anything." The void seemed like more than a coincidence. Instead, it sounded like the product of two disciplined men aware that police might be listening in. The silence, in this instance, spoke loud and clear. But prosecutors had more than circumstantial evidence in their arsenal. Pie Simpson had faltered. He didn't possess his uncle's uncanny ability to run illegal numbers profitably and without incriminating missteps. During their 10th recorded conversation, Simpson asked Adams to pay off a member of his gambling ring. There it was. Just a handful of indiscrete words by a two-bit numbers operator were going bring down the mighty Adams.

Adams's lawyer didn't attempt to rebut or reinterpret the content of the conversation. There was no use. It seemed as clear as the sound of their voices that the two men were involved in illegal gambling. Instead, Russell elected to challenge the identity of the man talking to Simpson in call No. 10. That's not Adams on the other end of that phone call, he declared. That's not his voice. Yes, that was Simpson requesting criminal assistance, but, no, that wasn't Adams on the other end agreeing to help. The state, Russell said, may have had the right guy on nine of the 10 recordings, but the wrong man on the tape that mattered most. By then, Russell knew Adams — and Adams's voice — about as well as any man could, having worked for and with him for a quarter century. One feature of Adams's voice was distinctive, Russell said. It rarely rose above a whisper. People often didn't realize that Adams was in a room unless they saw him because he spoke so quietly. While Adams's legend was enormous, the profile he maintained in public was so small that it bordered on invisible. Years later, Russell remembered an anecdote that perfectly captured Adams's modus operandi. A man from Washington, D.C., ducked into the Club Casino one day and went on at length, bragging about how he knew Little

Willie Adams. Russell said nothing in return. He just listened, and then he turned to Adams, who was standing just feet away, and laughed. The visitor didn't even recognize Adams. Russell's job in court was to prove that the state had failed, like the man at the bar, to properly identify Adams.

Russell had no time to waste. The trial would hurtle inexorably toward a certain conviction unless Russell could find somebody to convince the presiding judge that Adams was not the man on the 10th damning phone call. Russell couldn't rely on Simpson himself, because Simpson died after his 1980 conviction. Not knowing where to turn for help, Russell looked everywhere, scouring the country by phone in search of something he wasn't sure even existed: an expert in voice recognition. Coincidentally, his phone work produced a consensus and the man he needed worked right down Interstate 95 at the University of Maryland. The professor analyzed both Adams's voice and the voice on the tape, concluding that Adams did not take part in 10th recording. The caller in that conversation had more of a Southern dialect, while Adams has a "cultured black speaking dialect," the expert testified.

Russell argued that Simpson had been talking to George H. Boone, a furniture and appliance store owner in West Baltimore, on the 10th tape and closed his case. Boone, who had already been convicted of gambling conspiracy in the case, testified on behalf of the defense, saying he was the person on the other end of the line that day. He maintained that the two were discussing checks that he had agreed to cash for Simpson.

The state closed its case, arguing that Adams was the

man who pulled "the strings" in Simpson's illegal gambling operation. The defense countered, saying the state "manufactured" the evidence. "They ought to get an Oscar for fantasia," Russell declared, adding that the prosecution possessed "not one iota of evidence" to establish a connection between Adams and the conspiracy.

After five years of legal proceedings and a 12-day trial, Adams's fate, his future, now rested not with a jury but a judge, a 40-year-old Harvard Law School graduate with a penchant for bow ties.

At 2:15 p.m. on Tuesday, June 19, 1984, Judge Robert M. Bell, a graduate of Morgan State University and the Harvard University School of Law, dropped his gavel and raised his voice. Adams, Bell ominously intoned, has been "in a climate of activity that reeks of something foul." However, the state "has not shown beyond a reasonable doubt his involvement," Bell concluded, acquitting Adams of all three criminal counts.

After winning his freedom, Adams wasted no time exercising it. He stood up from the table, plunged his right hand into his pocket, whisked out of the courtroom and into the hallway, and awaited the elevator, all without saying a word. This was no easy feat. The courthouse was teeming with reporters awaiting the verdict in the case of Baltimore's most famous or infamous gambling kingpin. They scrambled to collect a comment from Adams, but he declined all requests, slipping out the door, down the courthouse steps, and into his car.

In need of some kind of comment to file their stories, the reporters turned to Russell for remarks. How does Adams feel about being exonerated? Russell answered honestly: "I don't know. He's obviously happy, but he moved out so fast. He wanted to get back to the office." Russell said he, too, was happy with the outcome, but he again alleged that police or prosecutors had manufactured the case and falsely accused Adams of being on the 10th call because it was their best chance of winning a conviction.

In truth, the state was correct about at least one thing in the case. The lead prosecutor at one point claimed Adams stepped into Simpson's gambling business to "bail out" his nephew when he encountered financial trouble.

Years later, Adams confessed to his role, explaining that he wanted, as always, to help out. His sister's son needed a job, so Adams first put him to work at his Pennsylvania Avenue retail shop, the Charm Center. Later, Adams gave in and set up Simpson in the numbers. He also provided counsel, including instructions about how to stay in the business. Adams mournfully concluded that his nephew wasn't very good at it. Adams didn't elaborate.

Did he serve as a drop-off man for his nephew? A drop-off man doesn't run a ring. Instead, he serves as a kind of insurer, taking on an organization's bigger bets or bets concentrated in a specific number where the payday could be larger than normal. Those closest to Adams maintain that he played no role in numbers after his exit from the business decades earlier. Regardless, Adams's reputation as a kingpin would not die, and it continued to haunt him and his legal ventures.

Regardless of Adams's role, the respected Baltimore newspaper columnist Michael Olesker bristled at the state's decision to prosecute him at the same time that it was operating a nearly identical lottery of its own. The state obviously could no longer make the argument that the game is immoral, he wrote. One possible justification for investing in the case could be that Adams used the proceeds to finance a drug distribution operation, as so many other racketeers did. So Olesker asked the authorities directly: did you turn up any connection to illegal narcotics?

"No," a prosecutor answered. "If we had any indication of that, we wouldn't have stopped the investigation .... This was strictly numbers."

Olesker's sarcastic one-word reaction: "Wonderful."

The verdict spurred public reaction, just as the initial charges did years earlier. Saying he was pleased with the outcome, Baltimore lawyer Dwight Petit described Adams as a "pioneer in the effort to bring the minority business persons together." Petit added: "He has been responsible for a majority of the businesses owned by minorities in the city to become successful, just by helping them get started."

Adams's family doctor, Uthman Ray, extolled him for fulfilling his responsibility to serve as his brother's keeper by giving "many people business directions and economic directions."

While Adams chose not to speak to the press following the verdict, he did sit down around the same time with a magazine reporter and spoke with uncharacteristic candor. Invariably scrupulous about presenting a tightly controlled narrative when talking about himself publicly, typically sticking with the line that he was just a poor little black kid with a talent for math and a commitment to black economic empowerment, Adams deviated during this interview. It is impossible to know now whether this, too, was intentional. Perhaps he felt that he'd gotten to the stage of life where he could afford to be more forthcoming. Or maybe he had just had enough of the state and the cynics.

"They say I'm a political boss, that I'm mixed up with dope and organized crime, but none of it's true," he lashed. "I'm convinced most of my legal problems started because I was the first black man in this city who could afford to move into a well-off white suburban community." But with that said, he snapped back to his well-worn lines. The revelations were over. "No one has ever made criminal charges stick against me, and no one ever will. I'm just a little black boy who was determined above all to keep some of the money white folks were draining out of the black community in the black community where it was needed most." Adams's interview sounded very much like a valediction speech for a career that had already spanned more than a half century.

028 DRAFTED FOR WAR

As Adams fought for his freedom, people associated with his real estate development firm, A&R, found themselves in a fight for their lives. On the first Friday morning of 1980, Adam Bantner, a superintendent for A&R's construction partner, Jolly Co., visited the location where his company was preparing to build 120 townhomes. He scouted the two-block construction site in South Philadelphia's Whitman Park neighborhood to determine where to position equipment and trailers for the work scheduled to begin in a matter of weeks. When he completed the assignment, he hopped into his pickup truck to make the 100-mile drive back to Baltimore. He barely made it 100 feet. At first, a single car occupied by a single person blocked his path. But within a few moments, the barricade swelled by roughly a half dozen women on foot, one of them making the group's intentions clear: You're lucky the men aren't at home. Otherwise you would have been beaten up by now, she said.

Despite the ominous warning, Bantner agreed to follow the women across the street to one of their homes. Inside, they provided an animated, acrimonious crash-course lesson to Bantner about the long-delayed Whitman Park project, wagging their fingers in his face all the while. They then put him on the telephone with the president of their organization, the Whitman Council, a community group dedicated to thwarting the development. "If you don't want to see bloodshed," Fred Druding informed Bantner, "you better stop" the project. To reinforce the threat, another member phoned Bantner's wife in Baltimore and helpfully explained the grave decision her husband faced. Nevertheless, Bantner gamely tried to win over the irate group clustered around him. I intend to relocate from Baltimore to Philadelphia for the duration of the project, he explained. Don't bother, they responded. Every real estate agent in the region will be notified and instructed not to assist you. But if you should prevail and secure housing, "You wouldn't last through one night," one woman declared. "You'd be burned out." Incredulous, Bantner asked if the angry residents had ever actually harmed anyone? "Not yet," they replied.

After another series of threats, Bantner relented. I am abandoning the project immediately, and I will advise my company to do the same, he said. Demonstrating the sincerity of his conversion, he placed a telephone call to his boss while standing in front of his antagonists. His supervisor later recalled that Bantner was "extremely shaken" and rambling incoherently when he called to urge him to walk away from the Philadelphia project at once. Although rendered under duress, Bantner's recommendation was a sound one. By 1980, the opponents of the Whitman Park development, fueled by racism, had successfully blocked the project — and the federal government — for nearly a quarter century. They clearly knew what they were doing.

Following the passage in 1949 of the American Housing Act, which paved the way for the development of public housing, government officials in Philadelphia decided to build publicly financed homes for their low-income residents. The first hearings for the initiative were held on June 4, 1956. Shortly thereafter, representatives of the local and federal governments signed off on a plan to build a 476-unit high-rise on the Whitman Park site, located a few blocks away from the Delaware River docks. But as the groundwork was being laid for the project, the opposition galvanized. And opponents felt little, if any, reason to dissemble about their motives. The project, they believed, would bring blacks into their neighborhood in large numbers and rend the all-white composition of their community. The group certainly received help from people in positions of power. Their congressman, U.S. Rep. William Barrett, added an amendment to the Housing and Urban Development Act of 1964, transforming the Whitman Park project from a high-rise tower to low-rise dwellings and slashing the number of units by nearly 75 percent, from 476 to 114. But even that was insufficient. They demanded changes from the developer hired to complete the project. Unwilling, the first developer dropped out. The Philadelphia Housing Authority then went shopping for a replacement and settled on a company called Multicon in the spring of 1970. When Multicon attempted to begin construction a year later, protesters blocked the company's crew. Scores of women gathered around bulldozers and backhoes and prevented trucks from making deliveries. Worse, it quickly became clear that no assistance would be forthcoming from City Hall or the Philadelphia Police Department. Without much of an alternative, Multicon sought to win community support by making concessions. As a sweetener, they increased the income eligibility requirement. Again, Whitman Council's members balked. Of the roughly 15,000 people on Philadelphia's waiting list for public housing, 85 percent were black. The income requirement wouldn't substantially reduce the number of black residents.

In the spring of 1971, opponents secured an even more powerful ally when Francis Lazarro Rizzo Sr. took the oath of office as the city's new mayor. Billed as "An Authentic American Racist" by the Philadelphia *Daily News*, Rizzo didn't disappoint. He wasted little time in shutting down the project, publicly explaining that he was fulfilling a campaign promise to the good people of Whitman Park. The authorities terminated the deal with Multicon, seemingly squandering 15 years of effort.

But just as opponents unified behind their view of the project, so, too, did proponents, who chose to wage their fight in the court system. In the fall of 1976, they prevailed when U.S. District Court Judge Raymond Broderick entered an injunctive order, requiring the local Philadelphia government, the United States government, and the Whitman Council to take "all necessary steps for the construction of the Whitman Park Townhouse Project" and to refrain from "taking any action which will interfere in any way with the construction." If plaintiffs harbored the illusion that their victory was final, their hopes were dashed when the defendants appealed, asking the second highest court in the nation to reverse Judge Broderick's ruling.

The U.S. Court of Appeals for the Third Circuit held arguments on June 6, 1977, and rendered a decision two months later, upholding Broderick's ruling, but with one critical exception. Yes, the government violated statutes and the Constitution and must therefore get back to work on the project. But the members of Whitman Council did not run afoul of the law, the court held. Consequently, the community group cannot be barred from protesting. Defeated, public officials had only one last legal resort, and they quickly sought it, asking the U.S. Supreme Court to take on their case. But on February 27, 1978, the nine-member court refused, denying the petitioners' writ of certiorari. Like it or not, they had to deliver. The only other option was no option at all. One branch of the government simply could not defy another. In the end, they did find another way to push back. They initiated another round of litigation that, like the first, went all the way to the Supreme Court. And for a second time, the justices refused to hear the case.

Having exhausted the legal system, the federal government needed to hire a developer to take on arguably the least desirable real estate project in the country. So they turned to A&R, the Baltimore-based firm they had dealt with successfully on a number of previous public projects. Familiar with the Whitman Park's tempestuous past, A&R's president, Theo Rodgers, made two unorthodox, non-negotiable demands. One, he wouldn't even consider the project without a one-on-one meeting with President Jimmy Carter's housing secretary, Patricia R. Harris. No deputy or underling would suffice. Considering the radical contract terms that he had in mind, Rodgers knew he'd need approval and backing from the very top. And two, he required a blank check from the United States of America. He explained that nobody could reliably predict how the construction process would unfold or how much it would ultimately cost. Consequently, he requested a deal with no precedent: a contract that would allow him to spend as much federal money as necessary to the get the job done. Without an unlimited budget, A&R would walk away from a deal unlikely to attract other bidders. Harris's staff attorneys strenuously objected to the proposal, correctly arguing that a contract without specific terms, without a specific dollar amount, was no contract at all. Whitman Park was to be a so-called turnkey project. In such deals, the two parties negotiate a price. For that price, the developer constructs the project and turns the keys over to the government when it is complete. The developer's profit is whatever amount remains after costs. If, say, construction bills surpass estimates, the developer suffers, not the government. Overruns can't be passed on. The government enjoys absolute cost certainty. Rodgers sought the exact opposite.

In Harris, Rodgers had a trailblazing counterparty. By the time he sat down with her, Harris had twice made history. In 1965, she became the first African-American woman to serve as a U.S. ambassador, and in 1977 she became the first African-American female cabinet secretary to the president of the United States. He also had someone with a tie, albeit a loose one, to his partner. Harris warmly recalled how she had shopped at the Charm Center, the clothing retailer owned by William Adams and operated by his wife, Victorine. A distinguished lawyer herself, Harris in the end instructed her staff attorneys to figure it out and finalize a deal.

Members of the Whitman Council needed no such directive to get innovative in pursuit of their goal. Undaunted by the string of courtroom defeats, they employed a variety of tactics to derail the project. For instance, they went digging for dirt on the city's new development partner, hoping to find unflattering information about the company and share it to provoke the government into reconsidering. Their research proved fruitful. They discovered that the "A" of A&R was, at that very minute, facing criminal charges for allegedly participating in an illegal gambling ring. Not so coincidentally, the information hit the media the day before a critical vote by the Philadelphia City Council in December 1978. On the day of the vote, the city and its lawmakers woke up to a newspaper article about the unsavory past of the city's new partner. "Whether Philadelphia officials are aware of Adams's background," the *Bulletin* reported, "could not be determined last evening." The measure passed anyway.

But the opposition did not relent. They argued that the pounding of pile drivers was damaging their homes. Experts found otherwise. Then they somehow convinced A&R's financial partner to withdraw from the deal. A&R found a replacement. They claimed A&R was spending too much, an audacious claim considering that they were responsible. The argument was dismissed by a federal judge. Then somebody attempted to burn the fledgling homes down, an effort the fire department both squelched and advanced, producing even more damage with their axes and firehoses. Some of the firemen were later indicted. And throughout the construction process, they tried to intimidate workers, constantly threatening them and hurling vile insults. Black workers were called niggers. White workers were called nigger lovers. A man hired to provide security at the work site later recalled how a regular demonstrator called him "scabby," "nigger," "dwarf," and a "50-cent prostitute" before trying to spit on him. When they weren't being serenading with epithets, workers were treated to a daily audio assault, as the protestors blasted the work site with songs and sounds with a high-powered amplifier. So loud was the noise that workers regularly had to abandon oral communication in favor of hand signals. In one instance, a worker suffered injuries during a concrete pour because an order to the truck driver to pull forward was overruled by a protestor speaking through a loud speak. "Back up," the protester instructed, and the driver did so.

So dangerous was the situation that Adams shared with Rodgers his safety concerns for everyone involved. The two men sat down to discuss the project and the opposition. Rodgers ultimately allayed Adams. However, he also recognized that A&R couldn't go it alone. By March 1980, A&R and the federal government had little choice but to ask the court system for help. On April 1, 1980, District Court Judge Raymond Broderick delivered. "We have now reached that time; the Whitman Council's recent threats and attempts to interfere with construction of the townhouses require this Court to enter an Order enjoining the Whitman Council and all other persons acting in concert with them from interfering with the construction of the townhouses."

The leader of the opposition, Fred Druding, responded, predictably, with vituperation. "If they build it," he said, "they'll have to bring in the National Guard — this is a 100-year war." The work site certainly resembled a war zone. The U.S. Marshals were called in to join local police in providing armed protection day after day, reinforced by helicopters circling overhead. As promised, Druding's allies did not surrender. In June 1980, they lay down in front of bulldozers. Seventy people were arrested.

Whitman Park finally opened to residents in the fall of 1982, more than a quarter century after the project was proposed. "I haven't had any problems," one of the first occupants reported. "I love it here," she said, despite the presence of a spray-painted message across the street blaming the "U.S. Govt." for its "housing failure."

A&R's Theo Rodgers didn't go quite as far as the resident in expressing his approval of the project, but he was pleased with the outcome. Not only did it prove profitable. It also improved A&R's already strong standing with HUD for future deals.

029 CULTIVATING TOMORROWS

Just as he had in his youth when he improbably rose from poverty to prominence, Adams continued to defy the odds in older age, maintaining power and influence despite his unassuming manner, overly credulous support of favor seekers, and, most significantly, the near-constant barrage of legal and business challenges, from his most recent trial to the travails associated with the development of Whitman Park. Despite it all, Adams remained in 1980 Baltimore's most powerful black man, *The Sun* newspaper claimed, stating that "the citywide influence of William L. (Little Willie) Adams, a power broker of long standing, continues." Although Adams conducted his business outside of the public eye, evidence of his influence could be readily and widely detected. Between 1969 and 1979, the number of black lawmakers at the city and state levels grew by more than 60 percent. And of the 12 black men identified in the article as the most powerful in the city, eight of them owed at least part of their success to Adams. For example,

Charles T. Burns, with considerable assistance from Adams, went from running numbers to heading the largest black-owned supermarket chain in the nation, Super Pride. With financial support from Adams, Allen Quille, Victorine's cousin, had become a dominant parking lot operator. And City Councilman Clarence H. "Du" Burns, with loyal backing from Adams, had emerged not only as Mayor Schaefer's chief operative but also as a legitimate prospect to become the city's first black mayor. All were indebted to Adams.

While it was relatively easy to discern Adams's influence, his holdings and worth were impossible to determine. During an interview with Adams, a newspaper reporter floated a figure: $40 million. Adams neither confirmed nor denied the number, explaining that discussing how much money one had was the equivalent of bragging. But the fact is that even Adams couldn't fully account for his net worth. He had money invested in hundreds of places and people. But the journalist gamely ventured a partial list: night clubs, taverns, a funeral parlor, and hundreds of acres of land, among many other things. At one point, Adams owned 11 properties in just one block of Pennsylvania Avenue, the 1500 block, home to his Club Casino and real estate office.

He had also recently added Metro Plaza, an office and retail development that helped to spur a major turnaround project that garnered national media attention in *Newsweek* and *Time* magazines. When a West Baltimore shopping center appeared to be on the brink of closure following the withdrawal of its biggest retailers, including Sears, community members called on Adams to do what he could to save it. The facility stood at the center of an area that had transitioned from white to black in the 20 years since its construction. As he so often did, Adams carefully assembled a strategic partnership to bring together the necessary expertise and influence. And again, he made sure to build an integrated team, believing in the power and value of diversity. He later joked that this partnership was made up of "one Jewish fellow, one Gentile and a soul brother."

"We needed the expertise and the know-how of people of all races," he explained. Adams then turned to the matter of money, and for this he tapped his established relationships. "Because of the confidence I had built up with white business men, we were able to raise the capital — $3 million through the efforts of my partners and myself. We raised the capital, renovated the building, and secured tenants." The new occupants included a mix of retailers and government agencies. The site, once moribund, blossomed anew and continues to flourish and serve the needs of the surrounding community. Adams ultimately sold his interest in the project to The Rouse Co., which integrated it into the Mondawmin Mall.

Following the company's successful development of Whitman Park in Philadelphia, A&R took on another charged endeavor. In May 1980, the first major race riot since the Civil Rights movement engulfed Miami, ignited by the acquittal of five white police officers accused of beating a black motorist to death after pulling him over for allegedly running a red light. The violence was particularly deadly and damaging in Liberty City, a neighborhood in northwest Miami where 18 people were killed and 850 arrested. The city's commercial district was burned to the ground, with the exception of a single building, a structure that had been designed and built during World War II by a man who feared that Germans would attack America's mainland. To prepare for the worst, he girded the building with poured concrete, an expensive material that certainly appeared excessive to many at the time of construction. When it came time to rebuild Liberty City, the community needed a redevelopment plan that would include a new purpose for the building that survived the riot. One of the people associated with the effort had come to know Theo Rodgers years earlier and called him in to elicit his assessment.

Rodgers shared his fundamental development strategy — draw on the stability of the government. If Liberty City could convince the state or local government to rent office space in the area, then it would have the anchor it needed to attract private-sector tenants. He also advocated for an aggressive sales pitch to a large grocery store. The community didn't have a place to buy food, and such a market would generate sufficient foot traffic to lure in other retailers. Don't even present your terms, he advised. You ask them what it will take to get them in your store. Both strategies worked. Liberty City secured a government agency and one of the largest grocery chains in the South. Shortly thereafter, A&R won the federal contract to build Edison Towers, a $5.5 million, eight-story apartment building not far from the building that withstood the riot.

On the personal front, all news was not good. The health of Irvin Kovens, his friend of 40 years, faltered badly enough for the federal government to release him from prison in the fall of 1980, just six months into his three-year sentence. Less than a year later, Adams lost his old friend Joe Louis to a fatal heart attack. Just 66 years old, Louis left life the way he entered it, nearly penniless.

Around the same time, Adams encouraged his wife, Victorine, to forgo a re-election campaign and retire. She declined, stating her desire to serve one final term. Near the conclusion of that final term, in the summer of 1983, she shared her intentions with the public. "This decision is a difficult one, because I loved my job," she said. But, she continued, "I did not feel I could measure up to a campaign this summer. I didn't feel I could sit still and get re-elected."

When asked if health issues were a contributing factor, Victorine said no. "Just like everything else," she explained, "machines wear out, and I'm wearing out and wearing down."

During her 16 years in the City Council, she disabused cynics who suspected she would do nothing more than her husband's bidding. Instead, she dedicated her career to protecting and empowering the disenfranchised. Victorine Adams recognized as few other lawmakers seemed to, or cared to, that urban poverty too often proved fatal. Unable to afford all of life's necessities, many in penury made the decision to let their fuel bills lapse in order to pay for food and shelter. Some simply layered up in clothes and shivered through the winter, despite being indoors. But others chose to generate heat in other ways, such as by opening gas ovens or setting fires. Both techniques claimed lives. Adams responded by creating the Baltimore Fuel Fund to help Baltimoreans keep their furnaces running through the cold season. Similar funds are in operation nationwide today.

Victorine did not, however, quit her commitment to

helping others when she stepped down from the City Council. In 1984, she and her husband established The William L. and Victorine Q. Adams Foundation. Still in operation, the foundation provides college scholarships to black students interested in business careers and invests in various educational institutions throughout Baltimore.

030 TURNING POINTS

William Donald Schafer may have owed his position as Baltimore's mayor to Adams's longtime friend and political ally, Irvin Kovens, but he had no interest in merely keeping his high perch warm. Nobody had bigger dreams for Baltimore than Schaefer, and nobody made more daring moves to bring those dreams about. It was Schaefer, for example, who transformed Baltimore's Inner Harbor from an unappealing and under-employed working port into a national tourism destination, throwing open the doors to the Harborplace marketplace in 1980. A year later and right next door, Schaefer opened an aquarium, a facility so grand that U.S. Congress granted it "national" status. His vision extended around the waterfront to Canton, a blue-collar enclave on the eastern shore. In this, he received a boost from a failure of sorts.

To make way for the planned construction of Interstate 95 through the heart of Baltimore City, the government acquired land along the designated route. But after Barbara Mikulski — then a little-known social worker who went on to become a U.S. Senator — led the successful fight to spare the city's neighborhoods and push the highway out to Baltimore's periphery, the government suddenly found itself with unneeded property on its hands and sought private proposals for development. A particular swath of land, a 6.8-acre parcel in Canton, drew considerable interest. The city received 10 proposals in all. In the end, Schaefer selected the firm headed by Adams and Rodgers to continue his master plan for transformation. Their proposal called for the construction of 133 townhomes and a park, all of it privately financed. A&R's prevailed, the government explained, by earning the community's support, devising a project that complemented other area projects, and by delivering superior design.

Privately, Schaefer urged Rodgers to build the most expensive homes that he could, reasoning that the new units would help to trigger a renaissance, attract higher-income residents who were likely to get involved in the community, and generate more real estate taxes for the city. Schaefer proved prescient, again. The units sold months before they were even completed and fetched offers that exceeded the original prices.

The work Schaefer did to refashion the city won him nationwide attention and turned him into a strong candidate for governor, a job in which he seemed to have little interest. Born and raised in Baltimore, Schaefer loved the city and rarely left it. But his political benefactor, Irvin Kovens, pleaded with his protégé to seek higher office. Schaefer ultimately relented and won the governorship. In 1986, Schaefer resigned as mayor to take his place in the state capitol, Annapolis. Baltimore's constitution called for the city council president to complete the term of a departing mayor, meaning Adams's friend and political beneficiary, Clarence H. Du Burns, took over.

At long last, Baltimore had its first black mayor. With his assumed term set to expire later that same year, Burns and Adams had to get to work immediately to retain the job.

As he had throughout Burns's political career, Adams strongly supported him. But it wouldn't be enough, as the city's top prosecutor, Kurt L. Schmoke, defeated Burns, becoming the first African-American to win an election for mayor. The 1987 mayoral election marked a turning point in Adams's career. For the first time since 1958, when the old white political boss Jack Pollack outflanked him with a black candidate of his own, Adams lost a race in which he was fully committed to — and invested in — one candidate. In 1972, George Russell lost his bid for mayor, but Adams had hedged, supporting both Russell and the ultimate victor, Schaefer. But here Adams went all in with Burns and lost. And it was particularly notable that he lost to another black candidate, backed by a new generation of black political operators headlined by Larry Gibson. It was not unreasonable to ask whether Adams's time as political kingmaker was coming to a close — or had already ended. Adams certainly wanted to close that chapter of his life. In fact, he expressed his desire to exit the political arena nearly a decade earlier. I would prefer to devote more time to my philanthropic work helping students to study business and economics, he told a reporter in in 1978.

Two years after his friend Du Burns went down in

defeat, Adams suffered another loss, this one far more painful. In April 1989, his longtime business and political partner, Henry G. Parks Jr., passed away at the age of 72, succumbing to complications associated with Parkinson's disease. In a newspaper obituary, Baltimore businessman Raymond Haysbert focused on his former boss's historic achievement: breaking the Wall Street color barrier by making his the first black-owned company to go public. "That's so significant," Haysbert said. "Public financing of companies is what America is all about. Underlining that achievement is that only three or four other black firms have followed Parks into public financing since 1969," the year of Parks initial public offering. Even as Parks was building and leading Parks Inc., he also served as a lawmaker on the Baltimore City Council, where, from 1963 through 1969, he championed legislation for racial equality, among other initiatives.

Six months later, in October 1989, Adams lost another close partner, as Irvin Kovens, 71, died of congestive heart failure. While Adams, 75, had forged close relationships with the younger generation that Kovens cultivated, Kovens himself was irreplaceable. That Kovens was a political force — not a political footnote — right up until his death testified to his fortitude, savvy, and determination. Kovens passed away after successfully fighting to have his federal conviction overturned. One unconfirmed theory is that Kovens wasn't satisfied with that, either. There are those who believe he pushed Schaefer to run for governor because Schaefer's opponent in the primary was Stephen H. Sachs, the former federal prosecutor who put Kovens behind bars.

Without his most powerful ally, Adams would now have to collaborate with others or go it alone. The first political test came in 1991. Clarence "Du" Burns still burned to be mayor. But this go-round, Adams urged his friend to stand down. Burns couldn't win, not even with his full support, Adams believed. However, Adams remained committed to doing whatever he could to help his friend. From the Schmoke campaign, Adams extracted a deal: Support us, and we'll take care of Burns with a job if, or probably when, we win re-election. But Burns was interested in only one job: Schmoke's. It was not to be, as Schmoke easily retained his office in 1991 and again in 1995.

Many years later, Schmoke's top political advisor, Larry Gibson, extolled his former political opponent. Gibson first met Adams when he was a young lawyer. Gibson represented the Congress of Racial Equality, a group of civil rights activists. When CORE's leadership decided to open a headquarters building in East Baltimore, they turned to Adams for financing. When CORE repaid Adams, he was surprised, despite the fact that they had a legally binding agreement. Adams was, by this time, more accustomed with people failing to honor their commitments. Crediting Gibson for this astonishing turn of events, Adams did business with Gibson through the rest of his life — in a remarkably unconventional way that was classically conventional Adams. The long line of black borrowers made their way to Gibson's office during the years, seeking money from Adams. Gibson suspects that Adams himself referred many of the people to him, perhaps as a way to generate billings but certainly as a way to bring someone into the deal he trusted — Gibson. What's more, Adams turned the process upside down. Lawyers for the lender typical draw up legal documents or at least review the terms. Not so with Adams. He had Gibson, the borrowers' attorney, perform the task and accepted agreements sight unseen. Adams, Gibson said, was "very unassuming, very humble, and very persistent." Even into his 90s, Adams was working hard to help others, calling Gibson as many as five times a week. In 1994, Adams called Gibson for a different reason. He rang "his" lawyer to ask if he intended to attend the swearing-in ceremony of Wayne K. Curry, the first African-American county executive of Prince George's County, a majority black county neighboring Washington, D.C. Now unable to drive, Adams hitched a ride with Gibson and Gibson's wife. "Will was really proud of Wayne. He just wanted to be there."

031 TRUST IS THE BOTTOM LINE

William Donald Schaefer may have relocated from City Hall to the State House in 1986, but his heart remained in Baltimore. Furious about the defection of the Colts, Baltimore's professional football team, to Indianapolis and concerned that the Baltimore Orioles might also decamp, Schaefer strenuously advocated for the development of two professional sports stadiums in the industrial area west of the Inner Harbor that had slipped into dilapidation, the same location where Parks Sausage had maintained its headquarters. Never mind that Baltimore didn't have a professional football team to occupy one of the two facilities. Schaefer believed that the stadiums would spur development and generate demand for real estate among businesses and even, perhaps, people interested in moving into the city. As he usually did, Schaefer got his way, and work began on phase one, Orioles Park at Camden Yards. To accommodate fans, the state pressed the city to construct a nearby garage in time for opening day in the spring of 1992. The company owned by his old friend William Adams and his younger friend Theo Rodgers, A&R, submitted a bid with a plucky provision. To do the project, the firm also wanted the air rights above the garage to build a market-rate apartment building if and when the market would support it. Like Schaefer, Rodgers saw possibilities where others saw only the present circumstances — blighted warehouses and surface parking lots. The west side had an institution that could slingshot economic development if significant improvements were made in the area — the University of Maryland Medical Center and the associated schools for training doctors and nurses. Health care professionals worked around the clock. Wouldn't they prefer to live nearby if attractive accommodations and amenities were built in the area? He bet the answer would prove to be yes, and built a garage designed to one day be topped by apartments. The garage was completed in time for opening day, and some years later, Rodgers filled the air above the garage with a 151-unit luxury apartment building, contributing to the emergence of a vibrant new section of the city connecting Baltimore's downtown business center and the University of Maryland.

At roughly the same time, less than a mile away along Baltimore's Inner Harbor, A&R went to work on another parking facility, Lockwood Garage, targeting downtown offices, restaurants, retailers, and tourists. Rodgers picked up Adams to attend the ceremonial groundbreaking. But when they arrived, Adams elected to remain on the periphery, standing against the surrounding fencing rather than taking his rightful place at the center of the festivities and dignitaries gathered. Rodgers took note. While he well understood Adams's preference for maintaining a low profile, he grew concerned about his partner's decision to remain on the outside looking in. After the event, Rodgers called Adams's wife, Victorine, to check on him. Victorine reported that Adams had been wearing the hard hat Rodgers had made for him for the event, emblazoned with his name, around the house, seeming proud of the project and his company.

A&R proved to be one of Adams's most successful businesses, developing numerous commercial and residential properties, including the completion of the nation's first Hope IV project, and helping to transform Baltimore's urban landscape for the better. Adams attributed the company's strong performance to Rodgers, describing him as "one of the best businessmen I've been with." Adams held Rodgers in such high regard that he entrusted him to be executor of his estate, no easy assignment given Adams's penchant for investing widely and without outside representation. Adams sat on a sprawling portfolio in need of a team of forensic scientists to reconstruct it all. But Rodgers not only accepted the assignment. He took it with honor, working hard to secure repayments that Adams himself would have dismissed as uncollectible. Rodgers also decided to collect something else, something considerably more valuable than money. Adams's story, his ascent from poverty in King's Mountain to eminent business man and generous benefactor to black entrepreneurs and young people, deserved documentation, Rodgers believed. His example on so many fronts — from business innovation to civil rights, from economic development to education — could instruct and inspire others, Rodgers concluded. And so he convinced his friend, mentor, and partner to sit for a series of interviews. Rodgers, despite sharing Adams's aversion to publicity, also took part in the project, discussing Adams the man and his contributions to business and society at large.

"Will's style is 100 percent trust," Rodgers assessed.

He invested so heavily in so many because he wanted to help aspiring entrepreneurs and professionals to succeed and, by extension, lift the entire black community. And he invested in people because he trusted them to conduct themselves as he conducted himself. The foundation of his conduct was being trustworthy, always making good on promises and living up to his word.

Adams built his entire reputation on unfailing reliability, Rodgers said. "Will's banker, he'll tell you that he'd rather have a handshake from Will than a contract from anybody else he knows." In fact, that banker, John A. Luetkemeyer Sr., the chief executive of Equitable Trust Co., said almost the same exact words years earlier. And when that banker passed away in 1998, Adams served as a pallbearer to the surprise of many who didn't know they were even acquainted with each other, much less close.

Of course, Adams had imperfections. So determined has he been to cultivate black business people that he frequently let emotion and sentimentality trump reason, Rodgers said. But clearly, his intentions were pure and socially important.

"I think Will suffers from one fault: That's being too kind," Rodgers said. "He's the only person I know that I can say that about."

Conversely, Rodgers said, "I would say his greatest

asset … has been investing in people."

In business, Adams's strengths and abilities are numerous, Rodgers said. "Will knows numbers as well as anybody. Of all the people I went to Harvard Business School with, I'd put Will up against any of them. … I don't just mean adding them up and recalling them. I mean figuring them out, the analysis. He's as good as anybody."

Adams also possessed tremendous vision, the ability to see the potential where others saw nothing or nothing but problems, Rodgers said, pointing, by way of example, at Adams's decision to assemble patches of land strewn by weeds and scraggy bushes and create the successful summer destination Carr's Beach.

He also recognized the power of strategic partnerships. Just as important, if not more so, he could build talented, accomplished, and diverse leadership teams, having earned the trust and respect of business people from all races and religions and backgrounds. Adams himself once jokingly referred to one of his partnerships in a speech as being comprised of "one Jewish fellow, one Gentile, and a soul brother."

Perhaps most significantly in terms of business, Adams was a forefather of collateralization, a business practice that some bankers corrupted decades later, nearly bringing about another Depression in the first decade of the 21st century. Adams didn't pool precarious mortgage loans and sell them off in tranches as others did. Instead, he staked his word and his cash, which he quietly placed in bank safe deposit boxes. His beneficiaries could then borrow money from those banks, seemingly without assistance from Adams, allowing them to establish credit. Adams actually did the same for his own company, wanting to demonstrate that he was borrowing from established and trusted institutions. He also extended the practice to political candidates. Adams would send office seekers to one his banks. Using a passbook, they would take out loans collateralized by Adams, all too frequently failing to repay the debts, leaving Adams on the hook.

Through it all, Adams struggled not with his past in the numbers, but rather with the perception some held of his previous involvement in illegal gambling, Rodgers said.

"He tries not ... he tries ... it bothers him. It bothers him. And I think part of the motivation for some of the things he does is to compensate for that. It bothers him. He can't help it. Anytime you go through life with all he's done and people still conjure things up about ...," Rodgers said, trailing off. "And if you look at it, there's nothing wrong with it. I tell people, 'okay, Will started a business that the state has now taken over and is making [millions of dollars] a year. Same business. Same business. And he had a better business than they had because he was employing a lot of local people in the neighborhood. The money stayed in the neighborhood."

Added Rodgers: "There is a segment of people in this city, both black and white, that thinks Will walks on water and the greatest thing that ever happened to Baltimore. Then you've got another group of people that thinks the worst of him. These people don't really know him."

The bottom line is this, Rodgers asserted: "If it hadn't been for black folks, he wouldn't be where he is. These are the people who placed their bets with him and who trusted him with the money. They trusted him when nobody else would, when he was 15 years old."

Rodgers concluded: "Will never forgot that."

032 THE WIND UP

William Adams frequently introduced the end of his stories with the expression, "the wind up is," an appropriate phrase given that some of his fondest memories were of playing baseball, pitching in particular, during his childhood. And so, the wind up is this. "I was concerned about blacks having something. It was instilled in me, I guess, when I was four years old." His grandmother served as the primary source, emphasizing education as the pathway out of poverty and to helping others.

Adams arrived at another fundamental principle in his youth that remained with him throughout his life. "Growing up, I knew I couldn't do everything by myself. I had to work with others."

And work with others he did, including his wife, Victorine. During an interview in 1996, Adams said that a shared desire to help others contributed to bringing the two together in the first place and to preserving their relationship for so many decades. He followed up the assessment with a half-century-old anecdote. She had such great concern for the children she taught that she routinely paid for and provided them with all kinds of supplies despite the fact that she was making just $100 a month, he recalled. Victorine's devotion extended to a daughter Adams had during a previous relationship, Gertrude, caring for her as if she were her own child.

So consequential were their many contributions to greater equality, economic empowerment, and education that then-Congressman Kweisi Mfume took to the floor of the U.S. House of Representatives to publicly thank them. "Mr. Speaker, I would like to express my appreciation to William and Victorine Adams for the enormous work they have done. Their determination to improve a community which some people have lost hope for deserves to be commended. Mr. and Mrs. Adams have shared their time, talent, and finances for several decades. I am very thankful to them and appreciate all of their fine works."

On Sunday, January 8, 2006, Victorine Adams passed away at the age of 93. The praise was immediate and universal. The former mayor and governor, William Donald Schaefer, bestowed his highest honor. Adams, he said, was "a very wonderful council lady" who "saved many a person from being cold." He was referring to the fund she created to assist the poor with heating costs. State Sen. George W. Della Jr., who served with Adams on the City Council, enthused: "The lady always looked out for people in need. Always." And one of the Adamses' long-time associates, Raymond Haysbert, described her as "one of the shrewdest people I've known." He added: "Her currency was the quality of the life of the community. That was what she dealt with."

A direct political descendant, Sheila Dixon, who would later become the first black female mayor of Baltimore, said of Victorine: "She really was in the forefront early on for many of us making the decision to get involved in politics."

In Victorine, William lost a wife of more than 70 years and a partner in pursuit of a better world. He also lost a champion known for her integrity, which helped to burnish his image. Victorine bristled when the media repeatedly referred to her husband's criminal past. In 1971, she felt compelled to make that point publicly, rising on the floor of the City Council to declare for the record: "I am the wife of Willie Adams," she said. "And his former status has been chronicled and pressed for years — over and over."

"I want to remind some and inform others that I carved out a niche in Baltimore for myself with my teaching techniques by dint of hard work," she continued. "My husband's encouragement and financial support were not handicaps, but I did the proposing, the planning, and saw to the execution of many projects." She cited as examples her voter registration drives in 1947 and her years-long campaign "in the political action area for black women."

Four years after Victorine's death, that of Raymond V. Haysbert Sr. followed, on May 24, 2010. Haysbert, whom Adams and Henry Parks brought to Baltimore in 1952, was eulogized as the elder statesman of Maryland's African-American business community. "Ray Haysbert was synonymous with the struggle for entrepreneurship among African-Americans at a time when it wasn't very popular," Mfume said. Mayor Stephanie C. Rawlings-Blake called Haysbert's death the "end of an era."

The mayor and others could be forgiven for writing the postscript to that era prematurely. It was not yet over.

On January 14, 2009, State Sen. Catherine Pugh, Councilwoman Agnes Welch, Theo Rodgers, and a lifetime's worth of friends, colleagues, and admirers gathered in the community room at the Roland Park Place, a continuing care retirement home, to celebrate the 95th birthday of William Adams. With the help of an assistant and a walker, Adams ambled in and quietly took a seat at the center of the party. Both the mayor of Baltimore and governor of Maryland sent proclamations, declaring it William L. Adams Day. As always, he spoke selectively and softly. Remarkably, he was still very much in possession of a calculator for a mind, solving complicated math problems in a mere pulse. Many of the gifts given were emblazoned by the pictures of the new president, Barack Obama.

After several rounds of warm stories and dishes of cold ice cream, he thanked his guests for attending, adding that he hoped that there would be more birthdays, more reasons to gather and celebrate.

William Lloyd Adams died on June 29, 2011. He was 97 years old.

Considering his longevity, it is no surprise that few of the people who knew Adams best attended his funeral. They had already preceded him. But the oral record he created and inspired is rich.

"I never forgot how hard it was to work in the cotton fields; that motivated me to succeed and help others," Adams said in an interview. Never desiring to be famous, Adams said he had only two ambitions in life: "I was just trying to be a good businessman and help black people get into business if I could." And despite his wealth and power, Adams's sympathies remained throughout his life with the penurious and largely disenfranchised — people just like Adams before his success in the numbers. "I was mostly with the little people, which was my preference. I didn't think the people at the top were doing much, if anything, to help blacks up the ladder. Back in those days, when some people got up ladder, they thought they were all God almighty — and didn't do anything to help others get up. Not many were up; but when they got up, they forgot about little people. I wanted to help produce more successful black people."

"Blacks, we have always been very sensitive, and we have reason to be sensitive because we have been called everything but the right thing," he said.

In helping others, Adams succeeded to a degree that is all but incomprehensible, said George Russell during a 2009 interview. "It's hard to estimate the impact that he has had on the black business community." Added Russell: "His contribution to Baltimore is immeasurable."

Also struggling to quantify Adams's impact, Raymond Haysbert once employed an analogy. Adams was like electricity, he said. We can't see electricity, but it is the power that makes everything go.

Dr. John E.T. Camper, a civil rights activist and physician, said: "The truth is, Little Willie [did] a lot for the black people in Baltimore. A lot of people would never have been in business if it hadn't been for Little Willie." What is more, Camper added, "He supported the NAACP, and he supported me in my efforts to get Negroes jobs. When I need money for these things, I went to Little

Willie."

Mr. Adams "has sponsored many," Inez Chappell wrote to the *Baltimore Afro-American* newspaper, "who are now somebody who would be nobody without his help."

The *Washington Post* referred to him in print as "a one-man Small Business Administration, lending money to other blacks and setting them up in business."

A longtime friend, Sam Stewart, called Adams the "godfather of all of us." He added: "He won't admit it."

Unlike the godfather depicted in books and movies, Adams did not exact revenge on those who failed or betrayed him.

When Adams died, he was owed even more than he was worth, according to both his lawyer, George Russell, and the executor of his estate, Theo Rodgers. Few people felt an obligation to pay Adams back, Rodgers explained, and Adams refused to fight for it either through the justice system or physical violence.

Ironically, one of the few issues to spur Adams to laughter was his losses. Asked if he would do anything differently if he had the chance, Adams once quipped, "I would demand that people pay me. When they didn't, I should have foreclosed. But instead, I let them transfer businesses to others in hopes that they could make it work." But he quickly dismissed the wistful tone, replacing it with a joke. "They owe me millions of dollars now, God damn it, some of them," he chuckled.

It was that self-effacement, as well as his commitment to the African-American community, that converted political adversaries into grudging admirers.

"On many occasions we have been on opposite sides

of the political issues, yet I have developed a tremendous respect for his political and business skills," said Howard "Pete" Rawlings, who rose to become one of the most powerful politicians in the state as chairman of the House of Delegates' budget committee. "Mr. Adams has been an extraordinary person who has made significant contributions to the empowerment of black citizens. I have a growing appreciation for the quiet and effective way both Mr. Adams and his wife, former Councilwoman Victorine Adams, have served [their legislative district] and the City of Baltimore."

As for the way he initially generated the money to invest, by running an illegal gambling ring, Adams had absolutely no regrets. Quite the opposite. "If it weren't for the numbers business, a black couldn't get anywhere. It was the only way you could raise any money. That's the reason [I'm willing to] tell anybody about the numbers. Whatever I did in the numbers, it was to help blacks all the way through."

What he did genuinely and sincerely lament until his death was that more didn't go even further. "I don't like that we didn't go all the way that we could. I've never been too happy about blacks not going and getting into business the way they should."

Adams was being unfair with himself. The man who never carried more than $7 in his pocket blazed a trail on Wall Street by helping to create the first black company that sold shares to the public. And his partnership with Theo Rodgers, A&R, has developed more than $1 billion in real estate. But he was even more than a benefactor and a businessman, said Rodgers, a man not given to sentimentality.

"The two of them, he and Victorine, are two of the nicest people who've ever been put on the face of this earth."

APPENDIX

In 1977, William L. Adams received an honorary doctorate degree from Morris Brown College in Atlanta and delivered the following commencement speech:

Today, you stand on the threshold of a new beginning which calls for a new and revised concept. This new concept is developed from astrategy for life or a game plan which will determine how you use what you have learned.

One fact of life is that life is a gamble. But you should weigh the evidence — study the situation, so that the odds will be more in your favor. Realize you can't beat the percentages. So learn the percentages and work with the ones in your favor.

Yes, I've missed many opportunities in my lifestyle as a gambler. But hindsight always has 20-20 vision. These missed opportunities were gambler's risk. If you want big gains you have to take big risks. Little risked, little gained! But big risks can mean big losses also.

So, students — graduates — as you leave Morris

Brown and face the battles — face the risks — face the gambles of life — you must make your decisions according to your game plan.

I had the opportunity to invest $11,000 in a Florida land deal that would have gained me $1 million in three years. I passed it up.

I had the opportunity to invest $50,000 in Caesar's Palace in Las Vegas, which would have grown into $350,000 in five years. I procrastinated until it was too late.

Students, pick out your plan for the next phase of your life. That phase begins today. You face an uphill battle.

It is not an impossible dream, but you have to establish your objectives, decide where and how you are going to get them and stick to your game plan as far as possible.

Your game plan for your life must be flexible. This flexibility must be based on a firm educational background.

The first thing I tell young people is to get an education. Knowledge is yours. You have that in your head! You can lose a million dollars but you can't lose the knowledge you have gained at Morris Brown.

That is something that you have. It is yours and no one can take your knowledge away from you, in life, in business, or anywhere else.

You graduates have that information. Information is knowledge, knowledge is power. It is not easy in this world to make a living. It is not easy to work your game plan. But you have been supplied with the tools. These tools increase your chances for success.

Having a game plan, having the tools, having flexibility, will make your chances for success much greater.

I have had to change repeatedly in trying to reach my goals. You project this; you project that. In the final analysis you make a lot of changes to accomplish that objective.

Sometimes you will find yourself up against a stone wall. You must be adaptable. You don't keep fighting that stone wall.

A sign of a truly educated person is one who can evaluate circumstances, then modify his approaches and methods. This is adaptability. This is flexibility.

Be flexible enough to go around that wall, go over that wall, or dig under that wall if what you want is on the other side of that wall.

It may be necessary to forget for the time being what's on the other side of the wall and make a drastic change in a great part of your game plan.

I have had plenty of sorry experiences in the business world where I stayed on a project too long. There comes a time when a harsh nitty gritty evaluation will indicate it's time to get out before you lose more time, more energy, and more money.

You can get into business and do a lot of wishful thinking but that does not accomplish the objective. At some point, a change must be make. Know when to get out and possibly to get into something else altogether. You must be able to read the road signs. Read them, evaluate them, and modify your game plan accordingly.

Some people think because they have prepared themselves and may have even secured a degree from Morris Brown, these people think they know it all. The think everything is ready for them and that everything will be given to them on a silver spoon. When the silver spoon does not materialize at once, they are at a loss. Don't cultivate that attitude. You must keep learning, taking courses, expanding your mind and your horizons.

Be prepared to use your hands as well as your brains. There is money to be made in the trades and based on the regional location, the kinds of schools and the variety of courses offered in the South is way ahead in this aspect.

Many graduates think because they have their diploma that they know it all, that they are smart, and they try to be slick. They think they can fool people and that everyone else is stupid.

Most of the problems I have faced in financing businesses have been with people. I tried putting college graduates into business and most of the time we failed.

I became involved with people who were not willing to sacrifice the time to be successful. They were not willing to pay the price to be successful. They thought they knew it all, and they were too lazy to work hard. They thought they were ready to be big businessmen. They tried to be hot shots and thought they were big shots. They did not take care of business and then the dollars went down the drain.

You need a solid base to get started in business. You cannot start off with instant qualification and instant success. You cannot overnight take your capital and spend it for a Cadillac and at the same time have all of the luxuries you want in life. Not right away.

The best example of business smartness and business sacrifice that I know of is the little Jewish store keeper. The store keeper started off with very little, lived over the store, put in long hours, was open on holidays, and sold a little bit of everything. He could hardly speak English. But over a period of time, he not only owned the store, but he owned the whole block.

The most important thing he had in mind was saving money, living within his means, and educating his kids so the kids could go forward and do better things in business.

Contrast this with most of our people. It may be because we have not had the business background. We have not been exposed to business as a whole. You only get out of a business what you put into it. Put in a little, get out a little.

Many blacks start in business and the first thing you know they spend the withholding taxes. They neglect to pay their income taxes. They refuse to report their sales taxes. They keep no records or very poor ones. They use money that does not belong to them.

When in business, Uncle Same is your silent partner. About one-fifth of what comes into your cash register belongs to Uncle Sam. When the Internal Revenue guys zero in, they are ruthless. They want their money. And if you can't pay it, they sell all you have and may send you to jail to boot.

Business calls for discipline. It's a nuisance to keep the records, to do the bookkeeping, to pay the bills on time, and to record all transactions but these activities are the required subjects you must master to be a success in the business world and in the academic world, as well.

Competition is business and business is competition. You graduates will face great competition. You will meet this competition from other graduates from schools like Morgan State University, Harvard, Columbia, Howard, Morehouse and others.

I do not consider myself to be a black man in business. I consider myself to be a businessman who is black.

We at Parks Sausage have an integrated business. Even though it was black-owned, we needed the expertise and the know-how of people of all races. Because we were integrated, we had plenty of markets that we would have missed otherwise.

At Northwest Associates, at Mondawmin there are three in our partnership: one Jewish fellow, one Gentile, and a soul brother. We have a large shopping center on 50 acres of land located in the center of the black community. Twenty years ago when this center was built, no one imagined it would soon depend on the black community for support.

National chain stores started with the venture, but they left. And when Sears closed, the whole center was threatened to be closed down.

I was called upon by certain segments of the community to help save and revitalize the shopping center. To do this, it was necessary to purchase the Sears building of 200,000 square feet. So we formed an organization called Northwest Associates, the Jewish fellow, the Gentile, and I.

Because of the confidence I had built up with white business men, we were able to raise the capital, $3 million, through the efforts of my partners and myself. We raised the capital, renovated the building, and secured tenants. We were able to secure contracts for space from 15 to 20 entities, consisting of state agencies, federal agencies, and retail merchants. This venture received national publicity from *Newsweek* and *Time* magazines.

I could not have swung this deal depending on blacks

alone. I have been able in Baltimore to gain the confidence of the financial world by living up to my obligations, paying all bills when due, and keeping my promises.

This was done with honesty, integrity, and ethical conduct in all of my lines of business at all times.

So we must integrate our business if we want to grow, if we want to deal in millions rather than in hundreds of dollars. This is an example of the new concept in business today.

Today is the day of specialization, whereas you should be able to do more than one thing. Specialization, however, in a field creates better chances for success.

I am mentioning my successes. I will not have time to mention my many failures. As a gambler, I put my losses behind me and headed for new fields.

Here is my philosophy — Little Willie's suggestions of how you can make it in the world today.

1. Acquire capital. In business, it would be money. In other fields, it would be skills and experience.
2. Specialize. Be the best there is in your field.
3. Be flexible. Be flexible with your game plan. Make changes when necessary.
4. Develop proper attitudes. Don't be smart aleck. Don't try to be slick. Be courteous. Be ethical. Be honest.
5. Attempt to integrate your business and get in position to work to the top where the big boys are.
6. Be willing to pay the price for success. This means hard work, long hours, sacrifice of superficial luxuries at the beginning for the substantial

rewards that will come later on.

7. Realize the world does not owe you a living. You owe it to the world to be productive. Because at Morris Brown your teachers and your parents have invested so much time, love, money, and energy in you, now you must pay the dividends by being a productive member of society.

8. You should make financial contributions to help others who struggle to get an education. Each of you, when success comes, owes a debt to help send at least one student through college.

9. You should make considerable contributions to charities as well as to churches. Political power and economic power go hand in hand.

I would like to [close by discussing] Matthew, chapter 25, verses 14-31: Again, the kingdom of Heaven can be illustrated by the story of a man going into another country, who called together his servants and gave them money to invest for him while he was gone.

He gave $5,000 to one, $2,000 to another, and $1,000 to the last, dividing it in proportion to their abilities, and then left on his trip.

The man who received the $5,000 began immediately to buy and sell with it and soon earned another $5,000. The man with $2,000 went right to work, too, and earned another $2,000.

But the man who received the $1,000 dug a hole in the ground and hid the money for safekeeping.

After a long time, their master returned from his trip and called them to him to account for his money. The man to whom he had entrusted the $5,000 brought him $10,000 for good work. His master praised him for his good work. You have been faithful in handling this small amount, he told him, so now I will give you many more responsibilities. Begin the joyous tasks I have assigned to you.

Next came the man who had received the $2,000 with the report: Sir, you gave me $2,000 to use, and I have doubled it.

Good work, his master said. You are a good and faithful servant. You have been faithful over this small amount, so now I will give you much more.

Then the man with the $1,000 came and said, Sir, I knew you were a hard man, and I was afraid you would rob me of what I earned, so I hid your money in the earth and here it is.

But his master replied, Wicked man! Lazy slave! Since you knew I would demand your profit, you should at least have put my money into the bank so I would have some interest.

Use what you have and make the best of it.

I hope my message and this advice will help the 1977 graduates.

ACKNOWLEDGMENTS

One of the many writers I deeply admire, Bill Keller, the former *New York Times* reporter and editor who now runs The Marshall Project, opined that "bookwriting is agony — slow, lonely, frustrating work that, unless you are a very rare exception, gets a lukewarm review (if any), reaches a few thousand people and lands on a remaindered shelf at Barnes & Noble."

Keller went on to recall his decision to abandon one book project for which he had already been paid an advance, requiring him to reimburse the publisher. He characterized the annual check he had to write to the company "not as a burden but as bail."

The great George Orwell, of course, said something quite similar, declaring: "Writing a book is a horrible, exhausting struggle, like a long bout with some painful illness."

Likewise, one of my professors at the Columbia University Graduate School of Journalism confessed to his students, perhaps too candidly, that while working on a book he frequently found himself staring out of the window, looking at manual laborers at hard physical work and longing to trade professional places with them. Really. Sincerely. Right this minute. Please, anything but another page, another paragraph, even another phrase.

Many a mirthless hour I have spent wondering why in the heck I chose to disregard Keller, Orwell, and my professor's grave warnings and take on a book. Why, on God's great green globe?

Well, it turns out that there are actually more good reasons than I can comprehensively enumerate here, but I need to mention a handful of them, all of them people, all of them important — and many of them dear — to me.

Let me start with the staff and supporters of the Enoch Pratt Free Library. Thanks to their dedicated service and generosity, the Pratt is a seemingly infinite repository of enlightenment, support, and kindness. To highlight just one of their many, many contributions, the librarians repeatedly helped me to locate resources and to read microfilm on an evolving set of machines, which is no mean feat given my lack of proficiency with anything requiring a power source. They supported me with unfailing professionalism and patience. If you reside in or around Baltimore City, I urge you to pay a visit. Take a kid if you can. Sign her or him up for a free library card. But be warned: after doing so, you should immediately take a step back to make room for what will inevitably happen next — magic.

Now for what I *read* on those microfilm machines. I am all-but-constantly lamenting the diminution of the press, particularly newspapers, one of the greatest loves of my life.

I cannot overstate how much I enjoyed being a newspaper journalist. The reporting and writing I found in those aging papers was almost uniformly extraordinary. The lengths to which they went to thoroughly and beautifully tell important stories both exacerbated my sorrow for what's been lost and recharged my optimism about what we can regain if somebody, anybody, can figure out how to sufficiently monetize it on the web. This is no knock on contemporary journalists. Generally speaking, they just don't have the numbers, the time, and the resources that our predecessors had. I'm more than a little reluctant to identify the journalists of yore who so impressed me for fear of omission. But I can't resist naming one, for his newspaper work is so bloody good: Antero Pietila. His daily newspaper coverage was worthy of publication between hard covers. Lucky for us, Antero continues to write. He recently produced an exceptional book that anyone interested in race and Baltimore should read as soon as possible: *Not in My Neighborhood: How Bigotry Shaped a Great American City*.

For those who want to learn more about crime and Baltimore, my friend Stephen Janis has co-authored two compelling works, *Why Do We Kill?: The Pathology of Murder in Baltimore* with Kelvin Sewell and *You Can't Stop Murder: Truths About Policing in Baltimore and Beyond* with Stephen Tabeling.

Speaking of inimitable authors and invaluable books, I could not have made do without David M. Kennedy, a person I've never had the good fortune to meet, and his magisterial *Freedom from Fear: The American People in Depression and War, 1929 – 1945*. I am no historian, as I'm sure the previous pages make clear. But Professor Kennedy helped me to better understand the world that William Adams inhabited and that shaped who and what we are today.

I also am grateful to Blair Walker, who conducted a series of interviews with William Adams, Victorine Adams, and several of their associates in 1996 and wrote an oral history about him. I drew heavily on his interviews in various places throughout this book. I highly recommend Walker's *Why Should White Guys Have All the Fun? How Reginald Lewis Created a Billion-Dollar Business Empire.*

The law — particularly criminal prosecution and appellate work — is an integral component of this book. I could not have negotiated that thicket without the contributions of many, including two very gifted lawyers, Teri Guarnaccia and Paul Pineau.

I owe considerable thanks to three of my best friends, James Drummond, Dan Ronayne, and Eric Stocklin, for all they provided during the production of this book, both directly and indirectly. James, for example, took time out of his exceptionally busy schedule, on a Saturday no less, to drive me to Gastonia, North Carolina, so I could conduct some research where Mr. Adams grew up. Dan invariably made himself available for lunch or dinner during my multiple research excursions to Washington, D.C., and he picked up more than his fair share of tabs along the way. And Eric, a gifted photographer, delivered well-timed and much-needed reprieves from writing, roaring me out on the Chesapeake Bay in his boat to take in the sunset and a beer. Okay, two. Okay …

I also have parents. Next topic.

Just kidding. My mother, Sharon, has known longer

than I have that I would someday write a book. She's been making this explicit since I was about 15 years old, stating over and over again her expectation that she alone would headline the acknowledgement section of any work of fiction or nonfiction. It was meant as a joke, I think; but such recognition is certainly deserved. I may look exactly like my father, but my constitution bears more than a passing resemblance to my mom's. As for my dad, I could not have had a better one. They don't exist.

Now, what can I say about Theo and Blanche Rodgers? Not enough, that's to be sure. I am eternally grateful to Mr. Rodgers for entrusting this story to me. Will ranks high among the most important people in his life, so turning this story over to me was no small thing. My appreciation for the opportunity and Mr. Rodgers's input is inestimable. And I couldn't have done it without his much better half, Blanche. She's the greatest personal cheerleader in the history of humankind, perceptive to moods and even unexpressed thoughts, and responsive in a way that is supportive, sincere, and thoughtful in the truest sense of the word — full of valuable thought. That I also get to call them my in-laws is a gift that I cherish.

Even better, I get to call their daughter, Marjorie, my wife. I am deeply indebted to her and to our daughter, Ellison, for the loving, fulfilling, meaningful life that I enjoy. I owe them far beyond my means to repay, although I will not relent in my attempt to do so. My hope is that they'll consider this book a good-faith partial payment in a currency they value more than money, one measured in rich denominations of learning and greater human understanding. If this biography of Mr. Adams sparks the imagination of even just one young person in Baltimore City, I know that Marjorie will consider us even. Ellison may want to negotiate a sweetener on top, say a trip to the zoo or a spirited game of Uno, but she, too, will ultimately conclude that we're … cool. My love for you both is deeper than the wine-dark seas.

My final acknowledgement: This book isn't worthy of William Lloyd Adams. Heaven knows that I worked hard and long (very long), but I can't shake the feeling that while I played the notes, I somehow failed to make music, to borrow an expression. Any and all imperfections, oversights, errors, and examples of outright ignorance are mine, all mine. That said, it has been a profound privilege to try and document the life of this truly fascinating and inspirational individual.

All proceeds of *The Call Me Little Willie: The Life Story of William L. Adams* will go to the William L. and Victorine Q. Adams Foundation, which generously supports education and other edifying endeavors in Baltimore. So, please, buy a few copies for your friends and family, as well as the young people down the street and around the corner. Will's story, though inexpertly told here, is sure to spark the imagination of at least a few of our kids and spirit them along a path of success that they never before dreamed possible.

It's all about having Will.

NOTES

001: The Reckoning

1 He had gone: David Margolick, *Beyond Glory: Joe Louis vs. Max Schmeling, and the World on the Brink* (New York: Alfred A. Knopf, 2005), 79.

1 Widely perceived as proxies: Margolick, 6.

2 Fight had yet another layer: Margolick, 6.

2 They broke with policy: Margolick, 177.

2 Drew some 9,000 people: Margolick, 260.

2 Earned just: Nicholas Leman, *The Promised Land: The Great Black Migration and How It Changed America* (New York: Alfred A. Knopf, 1991), 18.

2 Louis's final public: Margolick, 271.

3 Surveyed the activity: William Adams recorded interview with Blair Walker, 1996.

4 Rare attainment: U.S. Census Bureau 2000 Brief, Educational Attainment, census.gov/prod/2003pubs/c2kbr-24.pdf.

5-6 Black families owned: Ira De A. Reid, *The Negro Community of Baltimore: A Social Survey* (New York: National Urban League, 1934), 27.

6 Whites couldn't afford: Adams recorded interview with

Walker, 1996.

6 Even had bathtubs: Reid, 34.

6 He was disgusted: Adams recorded interview with Walker, 1996.

7 Ship repair district: *Baltimore Afro-American*, June 18, 1938.

002: The Kid from Kings Mountain

8 Who was 22: *Baltimore Afro-American*, June 1, 1954.

8 All but abandoned him: Adams recorded interview with Walker, 1996.

9 Blacks were lynched: Timeline of African American History, 1901-1925, lcweb2.loc.gov/ammem/aap/timelin3.html.

10 Cash and a cow: Adams recorded interview with Walker, 1996.

11-12 She blamed her husband: Adams recorded interview with Walker, 1996.

12 Do so with impunity: David M. Kennedy, *Freedom from Fear: The American People in Depression and War, 1929-1945* (New York: Oxford University Press, 2005), 19.

12 Cents in 1920 Kennedy, 17.

12 Prop up prices: Kennedy, 17-18.

13 Math supremacy: Adams recorded interview with Walker, 1996.

14 Cotton Field Willie: Adams recorded interview with Walker, 1996.

003: Baltimore Beginnings

16 Place of possibility: *The News American*, Nov. 28, 1971.

16 Secured a job: Adams recorded interview with Walker, 1996.

17 Claiming more lives: U.S. Census Bureau.

17 Weighing just: *Baltimore Afro-American*, June 1, 1954.

18 Waiting tables: Juan Williams, *Thurgood Marshall: American Revolutionary* (New York: Crown Publishing, 1998), 51.

18 Foreign-born parent: Kennedy, 14.

19 Wiggins went out: Adams recorded interview with Walker, 1996.

19 Dr. Thomas's Beach: *Baltimore Afro-American*, June 1, 1954.

29 Unemployment surged: Kennedy, 86-87.

21 Wiggins made: *Baltimore* magazine, Jan. 1979.

004: Apprentice Racketeer

22 Boundaries to observe: *Baltimore Afro-American*, April 30, 1938.

22 His numbers operation: *Baltimore Afro-American*, Aug. 20, 1938.

23 Designated territories: *Baltimore Afro-American*, April 30, 1938.

27 Treated myself: *Washington Post*, Dec. 8, 1969.

27 Candy store: *Baltimore Afro-American*, July 1, 1954.

005: What's in a Nickname?

29 Internal starter: Adams recorded interview with Walker, 1996.

29 Age or younger: *Baltimore Sun*, March 19, 1979.

30 Precipitous failures: Adams interview with Walker, 1996

31 Higher institution: Kathleen Morgan Drowne and Patrick Huber, *The 1920s* (Westport, Conn: Greenwood Publishing Group, 2004), 32-33.

32 Outer skin: *Baltimore Afro-American*, July 30, 1938.

35 Executive order: Adam Cohen, *Nothing to Fear: FDR's Inner Circle and the Hundred Days that Created Modern America* (New York: Penguin Press, 2009), 51.

35 Four-day federal bank holiday: Cohen, 70.

35 Cut off from his: *Baltimore* magazine, Jan. 1979.

006: A Banker Breaks In

37 See better days: Adams recorded interview with Walker, 1996.

37 The other side: Victorine Adams recorded interview with Blair Walker, 1996.

38 How neat, quiet: Victorine Adams recorded interview with Walker, 1996.

39 It nearly tripled: *New York Times*, March 4, 2009.

39 Fifth largest: *Baltimore Afro-American*, July 9, 1938.

39 Less than two people: *Baltimore Afro-American*, July 23, 1938.

39 Spent less than: *Baltimore Afro-American*, July 23, 1938.

40 Started derisively referring: Victorine Adams recorded interview with Walker, 1996.

40 Was in trouble: Victorine Adams recorded interview with Walker, 1996.

41 Launched an investigation: *Baltimore Sun*, Jan. 1, 1936.

41 Baltimore fighting: *Baltimore Sun*, Jan. 1, 1936.

41 Within two days: *Baltimore Sun*, Jan. 3, 1936.

41 Fund used: *Baltimore Sun*, Jan 10, 1936.

41 Including George Goldberg: *Baltimore Sun*, Jan. 25, 1936.

41 Also accused: *Baltimore Sun*, March 4, 1936.

41 Will blossom: *Baltimore Sun*, March 2, 1936.

42 Transpired in the black: *Baltimore* magazine, 1979.

42 Back then, whites: *Baltimore* magazine, 1979.

42-43 About the numbers: Victorine Adams recorded interview with Walker, 1996.

007: Investigation Launched

44 I was walking: *Baltimore Afro-American*, June 18, 1938.

45 Embedded in the exterior: *Baltimore News-Post*, June 13, 1938.

45 Family was jinxed: *Baltimore Afro-American*, June 18, 1938.

45 Very tired: *Baltimore Afro-American*, June 18, 1938.

46 Issued a ticket: *Baltimore Afro-American*, June 18, 1938.

46 Just one day earlier: *Baltimore Sun*, June 21, 1938.

46 Baltimore's clothing retailers: *Baltimore Afro-American*, May 14, 1938.

47 Refusing to hire: *Baltimore Afro-American*, April 9, 1938.

48 Theaters and places of amusement: *Baltimore Afro-American*, July 16, 1938.

48 Before sunrise: *Baltimore News-Post*, June 13, 1938.

48 Car escaped: *Baltimore News-Post*, June 13, 1938.

49 We start on Monday: *Baltimore News-Post*, July 16, 1938.

49 Took the note: *Baltimore Afro-American*, June 18, 1938.

50 Investigation, we believe: *Baltimore Sun*, June 14, 1938.

50 Allers granted: *Baltimore Sun*, June 14, 1938.

008: Mob Invasion

51 Bomb terrorism: *Baltimore Sun*, June 14, 1938.

52 Reassigned to the investigation: *Baltimore Sun*, June 14, 1938.

52 Without any explanation: *Baltimore Sun*, June 19, 1938.

53 Tracked the vehicle's: *Baltimore Sun*, June 16, 1938.

53 Town of Tamaqua: *Baltimore Sun*, June 16, 1938.

53 Gangland slaying: *Tamaqua Evening Courier*, June 14, 1938.

54 Returned home: *Baltimore Sun*, June 16, 1938.

55 No connection: *Baltimore Afro-American*, June 18, 1938.

55 Staked out his home: *Baltimore Sun*, June 19, 1938.

55 The Carrie Nation: *Extra: The Magazine of the News American*, Nov. 28, 1971.

56 Linked together: *Baltimore Sun*, Jun19, 1938.

56 Indicted for conspiracy: *Baltimore Afro-American*, Aug. 20, 1938.

57 Knowledge of the attack: *Baltimore News-Post*, June 17, 1938.

57 Claim 10 lives: *Baltimore Afro-American*, Sept. 3, 1938.

57 Join the fray: *Baltimore Sun*, June 19, 1938.

58 Editorial cartoon: *Baltimore Sun*, June 19, 1938.

009: Your Head, Please

59 Too stupid: *Baltimore Sun*, June 20, 1938.

59 I have read: *Baltimore Sun*, June 20, 1938.

59 Sought her help: *Baltimore Sun*, June 20, 1938.

60 Termination of commissioner: *Baltimore Sun*, June 22, 1938.

60 Called splendid: *Baltimore Sun*, June 23, 1938.

61 Up and down: Paul Sann, *Kill the Dutchman: the Story of Dutch Schultz* (New Rochelle, NY: Arlington House, 1971), 161-178.

62 Drawing close: *Baltimore Afro-American*, July 2, 1938.

62 Real democracy: *Baltimore Afro-American*, July 2, 1938.

62 Reliance on the rope: Sherrilyn Ifill, *On the Courthouse Lawn: Confronting the Legacy of Lynching in the Twenty-first Century* (Boston: Beacon Press, 2007), 29.

62-63 Set it ablaze: Ifill, 40.

63 Too much emphasis: *Baltimore Afro-American*, July 16, 1938.

63 Divert attention: *Baltimore Afro-American*, July 16, 1938.
63-64 Full swing again: *Baltimore Afro-American*, July 16, 1938.
64 Burned a cross: *Baltimore Afro-American*, July 16, 1938.
64 Practically all the money: *Baltimore Afro-American*, July 30, 1938.
65 First time: *Baltimore Afro-American*, July 30, 1938.

010: Case Closed

66 Max Weisenberg: *Baltimore Afro-American*, Sept. 3, 1938
67 In Chicago: *Baltimore Afro-American*, Sept. 17, 1938.
67 Newspaper article: *Baltimore Afro-American*, Sept. 17, 1938.
67 We don't tolerate: *Baltimore Afro-American*, Sept. 3, 1938.
68 Sentenced to three: *Baltimore Afro-American*, May 20, 1939.
68 You have to handle: *Extra: The Magazine of the News American*, Nov. 28, 1971.
68 Drawing fines: *Baltimore Afro-American*, April 22, 1939.
69 Ordered food: *Baltimore Sun*, June 22, 1939.
69-70 Tall as me: *Baltimore Sun*, June 22, 1939.
70 Dismissed: *Baltimore Sun*, June 22, 1939.
70 Registered in his name: *Baltimore Sun*, June 22, 1939.
70 Vitriolic column: *Baltimore Afro-American*, June 25, 1939.
71 Back-room deal: Adams recorded interview with Walker, 1996.
71-72 Pretty closely: *Washington Post*, Dec. 8, 1969.

011: Going Legit

73 Nation's illegal: Lawrence J. Kaplan and James M. Maher, "The Economics of the Numbers Game," The American Journal of Economics and Sociology, Volume 29, Issue 4, Oct. 1970, 392.
73 Feelings at the time: Adams recorded interview with Walker, 1996.
73 Resorted to assault: Adams recorded interview with Walker, 1996.
74 In his own right: Raymond Haysbert recorded interview with Blair Walker, 1996.
74-75 Two adjoining buildings: Adams recorded interview with

Walker, 1996.

75 Strategic partnerships, Theo Rodgers interview with Mark Cheshire, 2010.

76 Blacks having something: Adams recorded interview with Walker, 1996.

77 Greater success: Adams 1977 commencement speech at Morris Brown College in Atlanta.

78 Legal and illegal: Adams interview with Walker, 1996

79 Seed hundreds: George Russell interview with Mark Cheshire, 2009.

79 Adams met Henry Green Parks Jr.: Adams recorded interview with Walker, 1996.

80 To attract Negro: *Baltimore Sun*, July 27, 1975.

81 Professor suggested: *Baltimore Sun*, March 18, 1979.

82 Career flopped: Adams recorded interview with Walker, 1996.

82 Lending bank: Adams recorded interview with Walker, 1996.

82 Ground rents: Adams recorded interview with Walker, 1996.

012: Teeing Off, in Court

84 Contacted Adams: Adams recorded interview with Walker, 1996.

85 Off the tee: *Baltimore News-Post*, July 6, 1940.

86 Liked to wage: Williams, 77.

86 In December 1935: Williams, 75.

87 Larger front: Williams, 76-77.

87 Turned down Adams: Adams recorded interview with Walker, 1996.

87 Pay your lawyers yourself: Adams recorded interview with Walker, 1996.

88 NAACP in 1936: Williams, 94.

88 Houston tapped: Samuel Stewart interview with Walker, 1996.

89 Public recreational facilities: Marvin P. Dawkins and Graham C. Kinloch, *African American Golfers During the Jim Crow Era* (Westport, Conn.: Praeger Publishers, 2000), 138.

89 Why couldn't they: Dawkins and Kinloch, 138.

89 Didn't stand: Dawkins and Kinloch, 138.

90 Their effort inspired: Dawkins and Kinloch, 151.

90 Regular customer: Adams recorded interview with Walker, 1996.

91 Converted from: Adams recorded interview with Walker, 1996.

91 Didn't overflow: Victorine Adams recorded interview with Walker, 1996.

92 Headed to California: Adams recorded interview with Walker, 1996.

92 Sweet putter: *Baltimore News-Post*, July 6, 1940.

013: Investing in People

94 When I chose: Adams recorded interview with Walker, 1996.

94 He had the knowledge: Adams recorded interview with Walker, 1996.

95 Adams bought: Adams recorded interview with Walker, 1996.

95 Adams donated: Adams recorded interview with Walker, 1996.

95 Soaring 566 percent: Adams recorded interview with Walker, 1996.

96 Hands-on method: Adams recorded interview with Walker, 1996.

96 Crayton agreed: Adams recorded interview with Walker, 1996.

96-97 I've seen him: *Extra: The Magazine of the News American*, Nov. 28, 1971.

97 Persistently circle: Rodgers interview with Cheshire, 2008.

97 Beach home: Adams recorded interview with Walker, 1996.

014: Dawn of the Endless Pursuit

98 Marshall and others: Antero Pietila, *Not in My Neighborhood: How Bigotry Shaped a Great American City* (Chicago: Ivan R. Dee, 2010), 106.

99 Paid a premium: Adams recorded interview with Walker, 1996.

100 Powerful white establishment: *Baltimore* magazine, January 1979.

100 Police! shouted: *The Evening Sun*, March 20, 1950.

101 Cash from the bank: *Baltimore Sun*, Nov. 20, 1949.

101 Opportunity to break up: *Baltimore Afro-American*, March 21, 1950.

101 New approach: *Evening Sun*, March 20, 1950.

102 Winning an acquittal: *Baltimore Sun*, March 21, 1950.

102 Foolish notion: *Baltimore Afro-American*, March 21, 1950.

102 Forwarded their collections: *Evening Sun*, March 20, 1950.

103 Adams's wasn't one of them: *Baltimore Sun*, Nov. 16, 1950.

103 Regularly relocated: Adams recorded interview with Walker, 1996.

015: Birth of a Breakthrough

105 Roof over his head: *Business Week*, May 18, 1968.

106 Cunning financial strategy: Rodgers interview with Cheshire, 2010.

106 First got to know: Pietila, 125.

106-107 He never winced: *Extra: The Magazine of the News American*, Nov. 28, 1971.

107 Inconspicuous cars: *Baltimore Sun*, March 19, 1979.

107 Small patch: Rodgers interview with Cheshire, 2010.

107 Delivery trucks washed: Rodgers interview with Cheshire, 2010.

108 Adams continued: Adams recorded interview with Walker, 1996.

108 I'll sign it: *Baltimore Sun*, July 27, 1975.

109 Where they met: Haysbert interview with Walker, 1996.

109 Uncommon vision: Rodgers interview with Cheshire, 2010.

109 Bandstand on The Beach: Rosa Pryor-Trusty and Tonya Taliaferro, *African-American Entertainment in Baltimore* (Charleston, S.C.: Arcadia Publishing, 2003), 7.

109 The Drifters: Pryor-Trusty and Taliaferro, 87.

110 Too big to pass: Haysbert interview with Walker, 1996.

110 Too many ounces: *Baltimore Sun*, July 27, 1975.

110 Preferred to shop: *Business Week*, May 18, 1968.

110-111 Two-part initiative: *Business Week*, May 18, 1968.

111 Parks eliminated nearly: Rodgers interview with Cheshire, 2008.

111 Fortress balance sheet: Rodgers interview with Cheshire, 2008.

112 Honors, including Adams: Frederick Douglass Evening High School graduation pamphlet.

112 His humble demeanor: Evelyn Beasley recorded interview with Walker, 1996.

112-113 I wasn't so busy: Adams recorded interview with Walker, 1996.

016: Congress Calls

114 Do you solemnly swear: Transcript, Investigation of Organized Crime in Interstate Commerce, July 2, 1951 hearing.

115 Desperate for help: William Howard Moore, *The Kefauver Committee and the Politics of Crime, 1950-1952* (Columbia, Missouri: University of Missouri Press, 1974), 42.

116 Sought to position: Moore, 44.

116 Viewed the decision: Moore, 207.

118 Appointed Victorine: *Baltimore Sun*, Dec. 12, 1946.

118 Expected him: Moore, 66.

017: "Controlling Lottery Figure" Indicted

128 Threats of contempt-of-Congress: *Evening Sun*, July 2, 1951.

129 Clearly in contempt: *Baltimore News-Post*, July 3, 1951.

130 Less than a month: *Baltimore Sun*, July 31, 1951.

131 Discussing day one: *Baltimore Sun*, Aug. 2, 1951.

131 He wanted to share: *Baltimore Sun*, August 23, 1951.

132-133 Who asked for bail: *Baltimore Sun*, August 16, 1951.

133 Gambling thrived: Kefauver Committee Final Report, Aug. 31, 1951.

134 Pantheon of the nation's biggest: Albert Fried, *The Rise and Fall of the Jewish Gangster in America* (New York: Columbia University Press), 104-105.

134 Probably true: *Baltimore Sun*, Sept. 1, 1951.

135 Adams felt: Adams recorded interview with Walker, 1996.

135 Ethics were unimpeachable: Russell interview with Cheshire, 2009.

018: Self-Incrimination

137 Personally conducting: *Baltimore Sun*, Oct. 17, 1951.

138 Consented to hear: *Baltimore Sun*, Nov. 17, 1951.

139 Cut the lawyers: *Baltimore Sun*, Dec. 5, 1951.

139 Shortly after: *Baltimore Sun*, Dec. 5, 1951.

139 Their witness: *Baltimore Sun*, Dec. 21, 1951.

140 Sherbow rejected them both: *Baltimore Sun*, Dec. 21, 1951.

141 Urged him to rejoin: *Baltimore Sun*, Dec. 21, 1951.

141 Withhold his feelings: *Baltimore Sun*, Dec. 22, 1951.

019: The Gavel Falls, The Betrayer Calls

142 Day after Christmas: *Baltimore Sun*, Dec. 27, 1951.

143 Threw out their convictions: *Baltimore Sun*, February 3, 1952.

144 Filed suit: *Baltimore Sun*, March 14, 1952.

144 Decided to continue: *Baltimore Sun*, April 9, 1952.

144-145 Prosecution would be permitted: *Baltimore Sun*, May 23, 1952.

145 State's star witness: *Baltimore Sun*, May 27, 1952.

146 One fatal mistake: *Baltimore Sun*, May 27, 1952.

146 Stunning phone call: *Baltimore Sun*, July 12, 1952.

147 Issuing an order: *Baltimore Sun*, July 12, 1952.

147 Prosecutors supplemented: *Baltimore Sun*, July 18, 1952.

148 First met: Adams recorded interview with Walker, 1996.

149 Fantastically false: Adams recorded interview with Walker, 1996.

150 Court sentenced: *William Adams v. State of Maryland*, petitioner's brief to the Supreme Court of the United States,

347 U.S. 179, Dec. 16, 1953.

020: All the Way to the Supreme Court

151 Highest court disagreed: *Baltimore Sun*, June 11, 1953.

152 Hayes responded: Russell interview with Cheshire, 2009.

154 Two congressmen: *William Adams v. State of Maryland*, petitioner's brief to the Supreme Court of the United States, Dec. 16, 1953.

160 Black first: *William Adams v. State of Maryland*, Supreme Court of the United States, 347 U.S. 179, March 8, 1954.

161-162 Substantially enhanced: *Washington Post*, March 9, 1954.

162 Wife wept: Russell interview with Cheshire, 2009.

162 Approximately $43,000: *Baltimore Sun*, Dec. 6, 1954.

021: Seeking Political Empowerment

163 First Negro physician: Edgar L. Jones, *Toward Equality: Baltimore's Progress Report* (Baltimore: Maryland Historical Society, 2003), 12.

163 Recognized racism: Jones, 26.

163 All-white organization: Jones, 27.

163 Opening its stage: Jones, 30.

163-164 Disrupt the integration: Jones, 30.

164 Before the United States entered: Jones, 62.

165 Election day: *Baltimore Sun*, March 19, 1979.

166 Without representation: William Adams's interview as part of the McKeldin-Jackson oral history collection of the Maryland Historical Society.

167 More than a dozen: *Baltimore City Paper*, June 29, 1979.

168 Personally contributed: Adams recorded interview with Walker, 1996.

168 Defeating Melnicove: *Baltimore Sun*, Feb. 15, 1999.

168 Qualified candidate: *Baltimore Sun*, Feb. 15, 1999.

168 Opened the floodgates: Victorine Adams recorded interview with Walker, 1996.

022: Planting Seeds and Evidence

169 Sponsor of the 1954: *Baltimore Sun*, Jan. 19, 1975.

169 Grown woman: Adams recorded interview with Walker, 1996.

170 Price of just: *Nashville Tennessean*, April 17, 1966.

170 Make a difference: Adams recorded interview with Walker, 1996.

170 Received a tip: *Baltimore Sun*, March 19, 1979.

170-171 Burst into: *Baltimore Sun*, March 19, 1979.

171 Prison sentence: *Baltimore Sun*, March 19, 1979.

172 Slashing his own wrists: *Baltimore Sun*, June 12, 1958.

172 Guilty verdict: *Baltimore Sun*, June 11, 1958.

172 Illegally influence: *Baltimore Sun*, June 12, 1958.

173 Every dive: *Baltimore Sun*, June 15, 1958.

173 Would not stand: *Baltimore Sun*, May 13, 1960.

173 Additional convictions: *Baltimore Sun*, Feb. 21, 1961

173 Against Parks: *Baltimore Sun*, June 11, 1958.

175 Two strokes: *Cleveland Plain Dealer*, July 7, 1958.

175 Wrong person: Russell interview with Cheshire, 2009.

175 Preferring instead: Adams recorded interview with Walker, 1996.

023: The Backer Gets It

176 More progress: Adams recorded interview with Walker, 1996.

177 Migrated to Baltimore: Verda Welcome interviewed as part of Gov. McKeldin-Dr. Lillie May Jackson Project, July 8, 1976.

177 Turned on Adams: Ethel Rich recorded interview with Blair Walker, 1996.

178 Verda was elected: *News American* magazine, Nov. 1978.

178 Mobilizing black voters: *Baltimore Sun*, Dec 15, 1966.

179 I was mesmerized: Kweisi Mfume, *No Free Ride: From the Mean Streets to the Mainstream* (New York: Ballantine, 1997), 56.

179-180 Property damage: Peter B. Levy, "The Dream Deferred" in *Baltimore '68: Riots and Rebirth in an American City*, edited by Jessica I. Elfenbein, Thomas L. Hollowak, and Elizabeth M.

Nix (Philadelphia: Temple University Press, 2011), 5-6.

180 First disturbance: Levy, 6.

180 Eight undercover: *Evening Sun*, May 10, 1967.

180 Those days are gone: *Baltimore Sun*, Dec. 29, 1975.

180 He's tried to hold on: Terry Prestwidge interview with Blair Walker, 1996.

181-182 Frustrated by his: *Baltimore Sun*, Nov. 16, 1969.

182 Divide the organization: *Baltimore Afro-American*, Nov. 18, 1968.

182 Power to prevail: *Baltimore Sun*, Nov. 16, 1969.

182 Betrayed the true: *Baltimore Sun*, Nov. 16, 1969.

183 Economic growth: *Baltimore Sun*, Nov. 18, 1969.

183 Heart and head: *Baltimore Afro-American*, Nov. 18, 1968.

183 Damn town: *Evening Sun*, Dec. 31, 1969.

183 Fabled phantom: *News American*, Nov. 16, 1967.

024: New Blood

184 Proven a point: *Business Week*, May 18, 1968.

185 As a favor: Rodgers interview with Cheshire, 2008.

186 Act like one: Rodgers interview with Cheshire, 2008.

186 At a profit: Adams recorded interview with Walker, 1996.

187 Cost of the car: Rodgers interview with Cheshire, 2008.

188 A new client: Russell interview with Cheshire, 2009.

188 Judgeship to Adams: *Baltimore Sun*, June 23, 1966.

189 Oh, it goes: *Baltimore Sun*, March 19, 1979.

189-190 Not the right man: Adams recorded interview with Walker, 1996.

190 Among whites: Matthew Harris Joseph, *The "Sleeping Giant" Remains Asleep: Why Baltimore Was the Last Major American City with a Black Majority to Elect a Black Mayor* (Boston: Harvard University thesis, 1988) 116.

190 Last major city: Joseph, 4.

190 Deft candidate: Russell interview with Cheshire, 2009.

025: Execution Day

191 Anonymous caller: *News American*, July 18, 1973.

191 Chest and legs: *News American*, July 18, 1973.

191-192 The group: *News American*, July 18, 1973.

192 When informed of: *Baltimore Afro-American*, Sept. 15, 1973.

194 Allowed that some: Adams recorded interview with Walker, 1996.

194 Pieces of evidence: Stephen Tabeling & Stephen Janis, *You Can't Stop Murder: Truths About Policing in Baltimore and Beyond* (Baltimore: Baltimore True Crime, 2013), 107.

195 Various gimmicks: *Baltimore Sun*, Nov. 1, 1973.

026: The Sale and the Start-up

196 Another milestone: *Baltimore Sun*, Dec. 10, 1974.

196 Mr. Parks and I: *Extra: The Magazine of the News American*, Nov. 28, 1971.

196-197 Will is one: *Extra: The Magazine of the News American*, Nov. 28, 1971.

197 Run this business: *Baltimore Sun*, July 27, 1975.

197 First attempt: Reginald F. Lewis and Blair S. Walker, *Why Should White Guys Have All the Fun?: How Reginald Lewis Created a Billion-Dollar Business Empire* (Baltimore: Black Classic Press, 2005), 111-113.

198 Roughly 32 percent: *Baltimore Sun*, March 17, 1977.

198 It gets done: *Evening Sun*, Dec. 29, 1975.

198-199 Understand the needs: *The Zebulon Record*, Sept. 9, 1976.

201 Prison sentence: *Baltimore Sun*, Nov. 22, 1980.

201 His power makes: *Evening Sun*, July 17, 1968.

027: The Wiretap

202 Any investigation: *Baltimore Sun*, Sept. 27, 1979.

203 Supposed to react: *Baltimore Afro-American*, June 23, 1984.

203 Crazy to me: *Baltimore Sun*, Sept. 27, 1979.

203 Ally of Adams: *Baltimore Sun*, Sept. 27, 1979.

203 We were stunned: *Baltimore Sun*, Sept. 27, 1979.

203 Willie just couldn't: *Washington Post*, Sept. 27, 1979.

204 If I'm involved: *Washington Post*, Sept. 27, 1979.

204 Charging documents: *Baltimore Sun*, July 20, 1982.

205 Dismissal of the case: *Baltimore Sun*, July 20, 1982.

205 With the defendant: *Baltimore Sun*, July 16, 1983.

206 Wind up with anything: *Baltimore Sun*, June 8, 1984.

207-208 Turned to Adams: Russell interview with Cheshire, 2009.

208 Cultured black speaking dialect: *Baltimore Sun*, June 14, 1984.

208 Cash for Simpson: *Baltimore Sun*, June 14, 1984.

209 Adams and the conspiracy: *Baltimore Sun*, June 19, 1984.

209 Three criminal counts: *Baltimore Sun*, June 20, 1984.

210 Back to the office: *Baltimore Sun*, June 20, 1984.

210 Financial trouble: *Baltimore Sun*, June 19, 1984.

210 Good at it: Adams recorded interview with Walker, 1996.

210-211 Game is immoral: *Baltimore Sun*, Sept. 27, 1979.

211 Helping them get started: *Baltimore Afro-American*, June 23, 1984.

211 Economic directions: *Baltimore Afro-American*, June 23, 1984.

212 Dope and organized crime: *Baltimore* magazine, January 1979.

028: Drafted for War

213 Build 120 townhomes: *Resident Advisory Board et al. v. Frank L. Rizzo et al.* 503 F. Supp. 383. U.S. District Court, Eastern District of Pennsylvania. April 1, 1980, paragraph 18.

213 Beaten up by now: *Resident Advisory Board v. Frank L. Rizzo*, paragraph 18.

214 The project: *Resident Advisory Board v. Frank L. Rizzo*, paragraph 20.

214 Burned out: *Resident Advisory Board v. Frank L. Rizzo*, paragraph 23.

214 Project immediately: *Resident Advisory Board v. Frank L. Rizzo*, paragraph 25.

216 Authentic American racist: *Philadelphia Daily News*, March 28, 1978.

217-218 One-on-one meeting. Rodgers interview with Cheshire,

2008.

219 Determined last evening: *The Bulletin*, December 1978.

219 From the deal: Rodgers interview with Cheshire, 2008.

220 Later indicted: Rodgers interview with Cheshire, 2008.

220 Spit on him: *Resident Advisory Board v. Frank L. Rizzo*, paragraph 115.

220 Back up: *Resident Advisory Board v. Frank L. Rizzo*, paragraph 103.

220 And the opposition: Rodgers interview with Walker, 1996.

220-221 The townhouses: *Resident Advisory Board v. Frank L. Rizzo*, paragraph 92.

221 100-year war: *Black Enterprise* magazine, Aug. 1978.

221 Were arrested: *New York Times*, Nov. 28, 1982.

221 Housing failure: *New York Times*, Nov. 28, 1982.

029: Cultivating Tomorrows

222 Standing, continues: *Baltimore Sun*, March 18, 1979.

223 Floated a figure: *Baltimore Sun*, March 19, 1979.

223 Owned 11 properties: *Evening Sun*, March 11, 1971.

224 Soul brother: 1977 commencement speech at Morris Brown College in Atlanta, published by the *Baltimore Afro-American*, May 31, 1977.

225 Time of construction: Rodgers interview with Cheshire, 2008.

225-226 His three-year sentence: *Baltimore Sun*, Nov. 22, 1980.

226 Get re-elected: *Baltimore Sun*, July 2, 1983.

030: Turning Points

228 National status: www.aqua.org/about/our-story.

229 Superior design: *Baltimore Sun*, June 25, 1985.

229 Pleaded with his protégé: C. Fraser Smith, *William Donald Schaefer: A Political Biography* (Baltimore: Johns Hopkins University Press, 1999), 249.

230 Exit the political arena, *News American* magazine, Nov. 1978.

231 Go public: *Baltimore Sun*, April 26, 1989.

231 Conviction overturned: *New York Times*, Nov. 2, 1989.

232 Burns couldn't win: Adams recorded interview with Walker, 1996.

232 Extracted a deal: Adams recorded interview with Walker, 1996.

232 Young lawyer: Larry Gibson interview with Blair Walker, 1996.

031: Trust Is the Bottom Line

236 His company: Rodgers recorded interview with Walker, 1996.

236 I've been with: Adams recorded interview with Walker, 1996.

237 Much less close: Pietila, 127.

237-238 Investing in people: Rodgers recorded interview with Walker, 1996.

238 Soul brother: 1977 commencement speech at Morris Brown College in Atlanta, published by the *Baltimore Afro-American*, May 31, 1977.

240 Never forgot that: Rodgers recorded interview with Walker, 1996.

032: The Wind Up

241 Work with others: Adams recorded interview with Walker, 1996.

242 Their fine works: U.S. Rep. Kweisi Mfume's "Tribute to the Community Commitment and Dedication of William and Victorine Adams," May 16, 1991, published in Congressional Record.

242-243 She dealt with: *Baltimore Sun*, Jan. 10, 2006.

243 Involved in politics: *Baltimore Sun*, Jan. 11, 2006.

243 Over and over: *Baltimore Sun*, Dec. 14, 1971.

244 End of an era: *Baltimore Sun*, May 24, 2010.

244-245 And help others: Adams recorded interview with Walker, 1996.

245 Baltimore is immeasurable: Russell recorded interview with Walker, 1996.

245 Makes everything go: Haysbert recorded interview with

Walker, 1996.

245 The truth is: Dr. John E.T. Camper's interview as part of the McKeldin-Jackson oral history collection of the Maryland Historical Society.

246 Now somebody: *Baltimore Afro-American*, May 19, 1979.

246 One-man Small Business Administration: *Washington Post*, Aug. 9, 1971.

246 Won't admit it: Samuel Stewart recorded interview with Blair Walker, 1996.

246 Some of them: Adams recorded interview with Walker, 1996.

247 City of Baltimore: *Baltimore Afro-American*, June 23, 1984.

247 All the way through: Adams recorded interview with Walker, 1996.

248: Face of this earth: Rodgers recorded interview with Walker, 1996.

Appendix

249 Today, you stand: *Baltimore Afro-American*, May 31, 1977, and June 4, 1977.

INDEX

ABOUT THE AUTHOR

Mark R. Cheshire lives in Baltimore City with his wife, Marjorie, and their daughter, Ellison. A graduate of the Columbia University Graduate School of Journalism, Mark has worked as a journalist for the *Baltimore Afro-American* and *The Daily Record*, among other publications. He also has spent a number of years in public service, working as the director of communications for the Baltimore City State's Attorney and as the speechwriter for the Mayor of Baltimore City.